# The American Utopian Adventure

ICARIA

# ICARIA

A

CHAPTER IN THE HISTORY OF COMMUNISM

BY

ALBERT SHAW, Ph. D.

———

## PORCUPINE PRESS INC.
Philadelphia 1972

**Library of Congress Cataloging in Publication Data**

Shaw, Albert, 1857-1947.
    Icaria, a chapter in the history of communism.

    (The American utopian adventure)
    1.  Icarian Community.  2.  Cabet, Étienne, 1788-
1855.  I.  Title.
HX656.I2S5  1972          335'.9'77343          78-187462
ISBN 0-87991-016-X

First edition 1884 (New York: G. P. Putnam's
Sons- The Knickerbocker Press, 1884)

Reprinted 1972 by Porcupine Press, Inc., 1317
Filbert St., Philadelphia, Pa. 19107

Manufactured in the United States of America

# CONTENTS.

iii

# PREFACE.

A GREAT number of books and articles have been written in recent years discussing socialism and communism in the abstract. Some of these have been thoughtful and profound; most of them have a partisan tone, and are either in sympathy with the doctrines and projects discussed, or else are given up to condemnation and warning. The subject has been treated from almost every conceivable standpoint, and there would be no reason for the present monograph if it also undertook to enter the field of general discussion. Such is not its purpose or plan. Certainly the most common defect in the current literature of social and political questions consists in the tendency to generalize too hastily. Too little diligence is given to searching for the facts of history and to studying with minute·attention the actual experiences of men. In the following pages the attempt is made to present the history of a single communistic enterprise. I have endeavored to explain its origin, to follow the external facts of its checkered and generally unfortunate career, to picture its inner life as a miniature social and political organism, to show what are, in actual experience, the difficulties which a communistic society encounters, and to show, by a series of pen-portraits, what manner of men the enterprise has enlisted.

Whether or not such a study of a community now small and obscure is trivial and useless, must depend upon the manner in which the study is made. If made with the requisite intelligence and thoroughness, it may give a better knowledge of what communism really is and what it wants than can be obtained from reading abstract disquisitions about communism. Minuteness, far from being a fault, will be the chief merit of such a study. To be of any value it must be conducted in the true historical spirit. Truth must not be distorted in the interest of picturesque narrative. A didactic spirit and a conviction that communism and socialism in every form are dangerous heresies must not be allowed to make the investigator over-anxious to condemn or disparage; nor, on the other hand, should sympathy with good intentions and brave efforts lead him to a blind praise of projects in themselves useless or unpraiseworthy. I have tried scrupulously to avoid all preaching for or against communism, and it is hoped that no reader of the following pages will interpret expressions of respect for well-meant attempts to alleviate the condition of our fellow-men as signifying approval of particular projects about which I write without any distinct word of disapprobation. To speak well of certain men who participated in the Paris Commune of 1871 is not to justify that terrible episode.

There are two reasons in particular why this fragment of communistic history should be written. In the first place it is a story which, except in the most meagre and inaccurate way, has never before been told, and therefore it furnishes students of social science with a new bit of illustrative material; moreover, when compared with the annals of other communistic enterprises, the Icarian story is a peculiarly romantic and interesting one, and my opportunities for collecting the necessary materials have been exceptionally favorable.

In the second place, as an example of communism in the concrete, Icaria has illustrative value beyond all proportion to its membership, wealth, and success. Most of the communistic societies of the United States might better be studied as religious than as socialistic phenomena. Their socialism is incidental to their religious creeds. They believe themselves honored with special and direct divine revelations, and those revelations furnish them with governments of a theocratic character. They do not justify their socialism by any kind of philosophy of society, but simply refer the inquirer to a mandate received through their prophet or prophetess. I would not be understood as speaking contemptuously of these religious societies or their peculiar creeds; but I must insist that the experiences of such societies can afford little material to aid in the discussion of rational, democratic communism or socialism. For example, the Amana Inspirationists, a German communistic body, are to be found in the same State with the Icarians; and while Icaria, with its handful of members, has been struggling, in poverty and dissension, for very existence, Amana has numbered its many hundreds of people, has accumulated great wealth, and has lived in peace and harmony. And yet, for all that, the history of Icaria is as superior to that of Amana for the student of social science as the history of Greece is superior to that of China for the student of political science. Icaria is an attempt to realize the rational, democratic communism of the Utopian philosophers, hence its value as an experiment. The movement most akin to Icarianism was Owenism; but Robert Owen's colonies were all dissipated before their communistic life was fairly begun. Fourierism gained much prestige and made a considerable history in this country; but Fourierism was not communism by many degrees; and even those two or three phalansteries which developed most strength and lived longest, died very young. If then it is proper to distinguish what I call the rational, democratic community from the religious community (Shaker, Amanist, Rappist, etc.), which seems only incidentally concerned with the solution of the social problems which confront the civilized world, I must conclude that Icaria is the most typical representative of the former sort. Feeble and disappointing as its career has been, Icaria has persevered for more than a generation; and its experiences should not be left unrecorded.

To both Icarian communes acknowledgments should be made for courtesies and hospitality. Especially from Messrs. A. A. Marchand, J. B. Gérard, A. Sauva, and E. Peron, valuable assistance has been received. Many others have rendered material aid in the gathering of facts which were scattered almost beyond recovery. It may not be inappropriate to add that this study, which was first undertaken at the instance of Professor Richard T. Ely, of the Johns Hopkins University, has been accepted by the University as a thesis for the degree of Ph.D., upon the completion of a course in the department of history and political science.

Johns Hopkins University, June, 1884.

# I.

## ÉTIENNE CABET, THE FOUNDER OF ICARIA.

# ICARIA.

## I.

### ÉTIENNE CABET, THE FOUNDER OF ICARIA.

IN the year 1848, the readers of the *London Quarterly Review*, and also those of *Tait's Edinburgh Magazine*, were entertained with accounts of a contemporary social movement in France which had attained remarkable proportions and influence,—a movement which even then had reached its zenith, and was destined to be obscured and almost forgotten in the intensity of the political events crowding that memorable year of revolutions, and the years immediately following. The foreign tourist of to-day, as he passes through southwestern Iowa on his wonted pilgrimage from Chicago to the Pacific, may see from his car-window a forlorn-looking little hamlet of a dozen cottages grouped about a larger wooden building, the whole irregularly flanked with the unpicturesque sheds, stacks, and cattle-yards of a prairie stock-farm. Such is the Icaria of to-day, the humble survival of a movement which, a generation ago, numbered its zealous adherents by hundreds of thousands, and which assumed the mission of re-organizing human society with as pure an enthusiasm and as sublime a confidence as has ever attended the birth of any reform movement. The story of Icaria is a record of hardships, dissensions, and disappointments almost innumerable; but it is also a record of endurance, and of unswerving devotion that commands respect and honor. And, especially as heard from the lips of the few surviving pioneers of 1848, it is a story that awakens unusual interest and sympathy. Certainly no sincere and generous attempt to improve the condition of mankind, however disappointing in its outcome, is entirely unworthy the notice of the student of sociology or of the practical reformer.

The first French Revolution was essentially a political upheaval. Nevertheless, Voltaire, Rousseau, and the Encyclopedists, in their glittering doctrines of the equal rights of man, had propounded a philosophy which did not reach its logical ultimatum with the undermining of the Church and State of the *ancien régime* and the establishment of a political democracy. The emancipation of humanity, as preached by the doctrinaires, meant more than the subversion of kingcraft and priestcraft; it meant also a revolution in the industrial organization of society. The communistic conspiracy of Babœuf against the Directory shows the strength that communism had thus early gained as a practical creed. Marat, Robespierre, all the great revolutionary leaders were, in theory, advocates of the levelling philosophy. But it was not until the later revolutions of 1830 and 1848 that the socialists and communists took the leading part, and that the "tyranny of property" became a more pervasive cause of discontent than the rule of the restored Bourbon, or the republican "king of the barricades." At the period of the first revolution, the new philosophy had scarcely reached the French people. The masses knew that they were oppressed, but they had not yet imbibed the doctrines of the "social compact" and the "rights of man," nor had they yet learned that "property is robbery." But the revolution wonderfully aroused the intellect of the *proletaire;* and the nineteenth century dawned on a French nation of thinkers, readers, philosophers. It is not strange that ignorant artisans and peasants, severed from all the moorings of the past by a revolutionary cataclysm which effaced every traditional landmark, and stimulated by novel circumstances to an unparalleled mental acuteness, should have adopted the new social philosophy with the ardor of intoxication. If the revolution of 1789 was the work of lawyers, journalists, and men of education, those a generation later were genuine movements of the people,—though diverted from accomplishing the popular objects. The *ouvrier* had become a doctrinaire.

It is only by recurrence to these peculiar conditions and transformations of French society that we can thoroughly understand the career of a man

whose own life strikingly illustrates them, Étienne
Cabet the founder of Icaria. Cabet was born Jan.
1, 1788, at Dijon, in the department of the Côte
d'Or, his father being a cooper by trade. He had
the advantage of a general education under the
tutelage of his celebrated fellow-townsman Jacotot,
whose attainments as one of the leading educators
of the age, and whose career as a revolutionary patriot must have had weighty influence in forming
the character and opinions of young Cabet. Our
subject next appears as a student of medicine,
which profession was soon abandoned for the more
congenial study of the law. He acquired a speedy
reputation as an eloquent advocate at the Dijon
bar, and probably made himself well known as a
republican ; for, in 1825, two years after Charles X.
had succeeded his brother Louis XVIII. to the
throne, we find that Cabet has transferred his residence to Paris, where he becomes at once a leading
man in the new democratic movement which cul-
minated five years later. Associated intimately
with Manuel, Dupont de l'Eure, and other patriot
leaders in Paris, he became a director in the secret
revolutionary society of the Carbonari, which had
lately been introduced into France from Naples ;
and he threw himself fearlessly into the dangerous
work of extending this society and its principles
throughout the realms of his majesty the last French
Bourbon. He was an active participant in the July

revolution of 1830, heading the popular movement
as member of an insurrectionary committee. The
abdication of Charles X. was a triumph won by the
democrats, but they reaped small advantage from
their success. By superior adroitness, Lafitte,
Thiers, Guizot, and their coterie succeeded in out-
witting the democrats and in placing Louis Philippe
on "a throne surrounded by republican institutions." However, the men who had precipitated
the revolution must needs be recognized and con-
ciliated : and we now find our subject representing
the government of Louis Philippe as Procurer-Gen-
eral in Corsica. But Cabet continued to be a thorn
in the crown of royalty, and soon identified himself
so notoriously with the radical anti-administration
party that he was removed from office. Already,
however, his old neighbors of the Côte d'Or had
elected him as their deputy in the lower chamber,
and he took his seat with the extreme radicals.
This was in 1834. During his absence in Corsica
there had been incessant democratic intrigues, the
most formidable being the outbreak in Paris at the
funeral of General Lamarque, in the summer of
1832. The ministry had entered upon a course of
severely repressive measures, undoubtedly exceeding their constitutional powers. Cabet's opposition
in the chamber was intense. His denunciations
and predictions were too revolutionary to be tolerated, and the government allowed him to choose be-

tween two years of imprisonment and five years of
exile.   He preferred the latter, and found asylum in
England.

Hitherto, Cabet had been a man of action rather
than of speculation.   He had worked for the realization of a political democracy.   In his own life-
time, which had not yet spanned half a century, he
had witnessed a mighty growth of the people.
Under the reign of Louis Philippe, he and his democratic associates had secured an extension of the
elective franchise, and had seen the downfall of an
hereditary peerage and an upper chamber of aristo-
crats.   These political reforms had engrossed him,
but he had lived to see the popular movement shift
its grounds.   What had been at first a movement of
the middle class against an absolute monarch and an
intolerable aristocracy, had almost imperceptibly
come to be a movement of the lowest class against
the middle class.   The first and second estates were
no longer formidable ; Louis Philippe was the king
of the *bourgeoisie.*  Money was the new tyrant.  Capital controlled the electorate.   The government was
in league with bankers, manufacturers, and the mercantile classes.   Democracy now meant the movement of the *proletariat* against the *bourgeoisie.* Society
was breaking into two more and more clearly defined classes : the rich and prosperous, the capital-
ized class, numbered by thousands ; and the laboring
class, numbered by millions.   Oppression was no
longer conceived of as political, but as industrial.

During the five years of his residence in England, Cabet gave himself to study and reflection. His mental processes at this period are well described in a little French tract [1] by one of his disciples, from which I translate a few sentences: " Studying, pondering the history of all ages and of all countries, he at length arrived at the conclusion that mere political reforms are powerless to give to society the repose, the welfare which it obstinately seeks; that the slavery of antiquity, the serfdom of the Middle Ages, and the proletariat of modern times are, under different names, one and the same thing; that, in short, if the malady has changed its name it has not changed its nature. He found at all epochs the same phenomena : society sundered in twain ; on one side a minority, cruel, idle, arrogant, usurping exclusive enjoyment of the products of a majority, passive, toiling, ignorant, who remained wholly destitute. Excessive wealth and excessive poverty, such was the spectacle which every page of history presented to his eyes. To change all this, to find the means of preventing one portion of humanity from being eternally the prey of the other,—such was his desire, the goal of all his efforts. But how was it to be accomplished ?　*　*　*　Gradually this idea gained possession of Cabet's mind; he comprehended, he admitted that only equality of property could change the aspect of the world and

---

[1] " Icarie," by A. Sauva.

set humanity in the veritable path of its destiny.
The transformation was wrought ; Cabet was a
Communist."

Cabet was an honest man, with the courage of
his convictions. If his thinking had brought him
to an unexpected result, he did not shrink from his
conclusions. He had always ranked with "practical"
men, and he had no taste for being called a chimeri-
cal dreamer, a Utopian theorist, a *visionnaire;* but
nevertheless he resolved to become a propagandist
of communism as he had been a propagandist of
democracy. He was by nature an organizer; his
temperament was hopeful; his mind was constructive. When, in 1839, he was again admitted to
France, he had worked out his system of social reorganization ; and in 1840 the workingmen of Paris
were reading with enchantment the "Voyage en
Icarie." Cabet had wisely chosen to write his new
doctrines in a clear, popular style, and to give his
book the form of a romance. Little as the work is
now known or read, it is certainly one of the most
clever and captivating volumes of social philosophy
ever written.[1]

---

[1] The form of the "Voyage en Icarie" was, confessedly, suggested
by Sir Thomas More's "Utopia," and it contains many general
ideas common to nearly all of the numerous books describing ideal
commonwealths, from Plato's "Republic" down through the list.
But the "Voyage" is neither a plagiarism nor a mere imitation, as
several hostile French critics have pronounced it. Thus, Francis
Lacombe, in his "Études sur les Socialistes" (Paris, 1850), refers to
the "Voyage" as "copiée presque textuellement dans le Manifeste
des Égaux, dans l'Utopie de Thomas Morus, et dans la Vie de

The book purports to be the journal of an in-
genuous and adventurous young English nobleman,
Lord Carisdall, who has learned by chance that in a
remote part of the world there exists an isolated
commonwealth known as Icaria, in which the
government, the arts and sciences, the popular welfare and all the accessories of life have attained a
most astonishing perfection. My lord determines
to see the country ; and his voyage of inspection
gives title to the book. Part I., containing 300
pages, is an exhaustive and realistic description of
the social arrangements prevailing in this happy
country, as they appeared to a man familiar with
the civilization of England and France. Occasional
allusions to current European events lend an added
air of reality. Part II. tells the history of Icaria,
recounting the mode of its transformation and making an exposition of its doctrines and theories. These

---

Lycurgus." And Louis Reybaud in the " Études sur les Réforma-
teurs ou Socialistes Modernes " in a similar spirit remarks : " Ce Lord
Carisdall est en outre le héros d'un récit dans lequel Buonarrotti et
Morus, Fénelon et Campanella se donnent la main à travers les siècles.
L'Icarie est une terre promise ; elle doit ce bonheur au pontife Icar,
qui a un faux air de famille avec l'Utopus du chancelier d'Angle-
terre et le grand métaphysicien de la Cité du Soleil." It is true that
there are striking points of external resemblance ; but it should be
borne in mind that More's " Utopia," for instance, is a mere sketch
as compared with Cabet's volume of six hundred pages. In its
essential character the book owes much more to Robert Owen than
to Sir Thomas. It should not be forgotten that Cabet's chief object
was not the production of an original and unique piece of literary
work, but rather the promulgation of his new opinions in a manner
likely to gain the widest attention. For his opinions he doubtless
owed something to each one of the principal contributors to the
literature of communism.

new and superior arrangements are effectively contrasted with the vicious character of the former social and political organization.    Part III. is a brief *résumé* of the principles of communism.    Lord Carisdall, who is supposed to make his voyage in the year 1836, finds the history of Icaria to be somewhat as follows :

The country had been under the irksome rule of a long line of monarchs.    In 1782 a hero, patriot, and philosopher named Icar led a successful revolution.    Long reflection had made Icar a democrat and a communist.    He readily convinced his grateful countrymen of the superiority of his proposed method of reconstruction, and his plans were adopted with enthusiasm.    Ultimately, the country would become radically and exclusively socialistic; but the transition was to be a gradual one, occupying fully fifty years.    The government was to become at once a democratic republic.    The country was accordingly divided into a hundred provinces, and each province into ten communes.    Each commune was a small self-governing democracy.    Each province had its assembly composed of representatives of the communes, and the nation had its larger assembly composed of representatives of the provinces.    At the head of administration there was an elective executive council, of which the good Icar reluctantly consented to be President.    During the transitory *régime* existing proprietors and vested rights were to remain undisturbed, but the state was to begin at once a system of national workshops, tenements for workingmen, and various other ameliorations. Taxation was to be removed from all articles of necessity, and a graduated income tax was to be an important means of arriving at equality. So speedily as possible the public lands were to be colonized by the poor, and devoted to the application of thorough-going communistic principles, being transformed into farms and villages organized on the industrial model of the ultimate Icarian constitution. Meanwhile, great attention was to be given to education. This was to be compulsory, thorough, and practical, and was to fit the growing generation for the dawning era of perfect equality and fraternity. By the absorption of inheritances under an extended law of escheat, by the mode of imposing taxes, by the legal regulation of wages, and by the development of large national industries, the state would absorb all private property and all industrial and social functions, so that, at the end of half a century, the people would find themselves transformed into a vast partnership—a great national hive, where each labored according to his abilities and consumed according to his necessities; where crime had vanished with poverty, and idleness with luxurious wealth; where peace and plenty, liberty and equality, virtue and intelligence, reigned supreme. Thus the former *political* unit of the commune would have developed by a gradual and simple process into the unit of social and industrial coöperation. The waste of competition would have been replaced by the economy of general organization. Buying and selling and all monetary operations would obviously have become obsolete. Such is a slight outline of Cabet's elaborate "transitory constitution." The author was particularly proud of this portion of his work, which he believed contained many original suggestions and constituted his most valuable contribution to communistic thought. He makes one of the characters in the romance express regret that France had not adopted such a constitution after the July revolution of 1830.

The English voyager arrived in Icaria several years after the transitory period had been completed, and he found the system in full operation. Space will not permit us to describe the interesting and beneficent manner in which the Icarians managed to provide all their people with healthful and abundant food, pleasant raiment and comfortable homes—suffice it to say that Icaria was a veritable housekeeper's paradise. The educational system was admirable, and is elaborately described by Lord Carisdall. The organization of industry was ingeniously planned and effectively carried out. Hygienic arrangements of all kinds were beyond praise. Writers, savants, men of high and varied attainments had honored places in the system. The standard of morality was pure and lofty. Marriage and the family were deemed sacred. The position of woman was fully on the par with that of man. The treatment of women and children is a cardinal subject in the Icarian philosophy, and one will search in vain to find more sensible, enlightened views. The religious beliefs of Icaria were peculiar. All religions were freely tolerated, but the current belief was a species of rationalistic theism. (Cabet himself had a strong leaning toward Comte's positive philosophy.)

The second part of the book has a discussion of the faults of the old social and political organization, much in the vein of recent writers like Henry George. A valuable summary showing the progress of democracy in all ages and all countries crowds sixty pages with historical facts. Next follows a brief historical sketch of industrial progress. And, above all, comes finally a sort of chronological cyclopedia of communistic philosophers, bristling with names like those of Pythagoras, Lycurgus, Socrates, Plato, the Gracchi, Plutarch, the Fathers of the Church, Sir Thomas More, Fénélon, Grotius, Hobbes, Harrington, John Locke, Campanella, Rousseau, Morelly, Babœuf, Buonarotti, Robert Owen, Saint-Simon, Fourier, and scores of others, all of whom are most ingeniously quoted as advocates of the doctrines of human equality. This plan of associating a purely imaginary picture of an ideal society, with so learned and comprehensive an array of historical facts and distinguished philosophers, was well contrived to give the whole work an appearance of verity and sober weight.   As Cabet says in his preface, the " Voyage en Icarie " is indeed "a veritable treatise on morals, philosophy, social and political economy, the fruit of long labors, immense researches, and constant meditations."   And he adds :  " To understand it well, it will not suffice to read the book ; it must be re-read, read often, and studied."

The title-page, in an elaborate and symmetrical arrangement of mottoes, contains a summation of all Cabet's philosophy.   It is so curious that I think it worth while to reproduce it in full upon the adjoining page.   It is transcribed from a copy of the fifth edition, published in 1848.

Such was the book which Cabet presented to the French public in 1840, and it met with a reception more immediate, and more serious, probably, than has ever been accorded to any similar work.   It suited the popular mind because it furnished a programme.   It was easy to read and to understand. Its generalizations were clear, and yet seemed profoundly wise.   Its morality appealed to the best motives, and satisfied the ideals of the conscientious. Though rejecting Christianity as divine, it accorded Christ the highest place of honor as a teacher

# VOYAGE

en

# ICARIE

par

## M. CABET.

---

## FRATERNITÉ

Tous pour chacun        Chacun pour tous

| | | |
|---|---|---|
| SOLIDARITÉ | AMOUR | ÉDUCATION |
| ÉGALITÉ—LIBERTÉ | JUSTICE | INTELLIGENCE—RAISON |
| ÉLIGIBILITÉ | SECOURS MUTUEL | MORALITÉ |
| UNITÉ | ASSURANCE UNIVERSELLE | ORDRE |
| PAIX | ORGANIZATION DU TRAVAIL | UNION |
| — | MACHINES AU PROFIT DE TOUS | — |
| | AUGMENTATION DE LA PRODUCTION | |
| | RÉPARTITION ÉQUITABLE DES PRODUITS | |
| | SUPPRESSION DE LA MISÈRE | |
| | AMELIORATIONS CROISSANTES | |
| Premier droit | MARIAGE ET FAMILLE | Premier deboir |
| Vibre | PROGRÈS CONTINUEL | Trabailler |
| — | ABONDANCE | — |
| A CHACUN | ARTS | DE CHACUN |
| SUIVANT SES BESOINS | | SUIVANT SES FORCES |

## BONHEUR COMMUN

---

PARIS

AU BUREAU DU POPULAIRE RUE JEAN-JACQUES-ROUSSEAU, 14
Dans les Departments et à l'Étranger chez les Correspondants du Populaire.

1848

17

of human brotherhood, of unselfishness, of equality, and of community.

The air was already full of social discontent. Babouvism had never wholly died out. Only the year before our book appeared the insurrection of Blanqui and Barbès had been recognized as a socialistic revolt. Fourierism and Saint-Simonism had each its large body of disciples. But nothing as yet had crystallized the vague longings of the masses. Icarianism met the situation. It was hailed as a new gospel to the poor. The "Voyage" was read not only in Paris but throughout France ; and it circulated widely in foreign countries, running through a number of editions.[1]

In the following year, 1841, Cabet founded a journal, the *Populaire*, in which he defended and expounded his ideas as set forth in the "Voyage." From 1843 to 1847 he printed an Icarian almanac, and a perfect flood of controversial pamphlets. During the same year he published his work on Christianity, and a "Popular History of the French Revolutions from 1789 to 1830," in five volumes, and he had now added the reputation of a man of letters to that of a radical politician. His "Christianity" ("Le Vrai Christianisme suivant Jesus-Christ") is a curious little volume of over six

---

[1] An English reviewer remarked in 1848 : "It has already gone through five editions—there is not a shop or stall in Paris where copies are not in readiness for a constant influx of purchasers—hardly a drawing-room table on which it is not to be seen."

hundred very small pages. It undertakes to set primitive Christianity in contrast with modern ecclesiasticism, and displays much ingenuity in making it to appear that the mission of Christ was to establish social equality among men, and that Christ was the chief teacher of communism that the world has ever seen. The newspaper, the almanac, the pamphlets, and the books were eagerly read and circulated, and no propaganda ever won a more immediate success. It is said on good authority that in 1847 the adherents of the Icarian doctrine—the members of the so-called "Icarian school"—numbered four hundred thousand, besides many more who sympathized with the movement. These were almost exclusively working people, especially the better class of artisans in the towns. So extensive a movement could not but attract wide attention and could not hope to escape prosecution. The press, the government, through all its organs of magistrature and police, the priests, and the powerful influence of the *bourgeoisie*—the mercantile class—were combined to crush out so dangerous a social heresy.

It is altogether improbable that Cabet had at the outset any design of putting his theories into immediate practice, or of demonstrating their feasibility by means of an experimental colony. But as persecution and controversy increased, his sanguine friends on the one hand and his taunting enemies on

the other constrained him into a project for the
realization and vindication of his Icaria.   He had
at first been content to hope that at some political
crisis the French people would be persuaded to organize a democratic republic, with a constitution
providing for a gradual transition to communism.
But now he was urged to found a colony whose success would be the best Icarian argument, and would
react inevitably upon the structure of European society.   Cabet had won the perfect, unlimited confidence of his adherents, and he had but to propose
the project of a colony to meet with prompt responses from large numbers who were willing to go.
Cabet was to them what the good Icar in the romance was to the grateful people who took his
name.

It was in May, 1847, that there appeared in the
*Populaire* a long oratorical proclamation headed,
" Allons en Icarie ! " (Let us go to Icaria !) and
signed " Cabet."   The article is now before me as I
write.   It sets forth in the most lofty and glowing
terms the desirability of an Icarian emigration.   It
promises a " new terrestrial paradise."   Moreover,
it expatiates on the unparalleled opportunity for
achieving undying fame and for winning happiness,
which should extend its blessings to the universe.
For a glowing prospectus this certainly surpasses
the best recent efforts of the Dakota land-agents.
It promised a heavenly climate, a soil that would

produce, with scarcely any labor, an unparalleled
fruitage, and, in short, every thing was to be magnificent—perfect.   But this first appeal did not
name the location of the new land of promise.   In
the next number of the *Populaire* he completes his
appeal, under the title : " Travailleurs, allons en
Icarie ! "   This address to laboring men sets forth
in strong contrast their unhappy lot in France and
the delightful life that awaits them in Icaria.   It
ends with these words : " Let us found Icaria in
America ! "   The next week an address to women
appears in the *Populaire*, inviting them to an eman-
cipated life in happy Icaria.   Only a few weeks had
elapsed when Cabet was able to announce : [1] " To-day,
after the reports and letters we have received, the
accession to our proposal is so prodigious that *we
have no doubt of being able to unite more than a million of co-operators !* "

Cabet had announced that a year would be required for preparations, but the people were becoming impatient to go.   The *Populaire* from time
to time drew flattering pictures of the success of
various communistic ventures in America.   It was
at this time that the Rappists in Pennsylvania were
at their zenith ; the Zoarite community in Ohio was
flourishing ; Robert Owen had failed at New Harmony, but he was still indefatigably engaged in
socialistic enterprises.   This was the era of the

---

[1] For the use of valuable documents and materials, from which this
portion of my sketch is prepared, I am indebted to J. B. Gérard.

Brook Farm experiment, which enlisted such names
as those of Ripley, Margaret Fuller, Hawthorne,
Channing, Dana, and others as well known.   I find
in a copy of the *Populaire*, in the summer of 1847,
a quaint little notice of " Brouck-Tarm, sous la
direction du prédicateur unitaire Ripley." The
*Populaire* was also kept crowded with letters enthusiastically endorsing the plan of emigration.
Preparations were making, but the destination of
the colony was not yet announced.   In September
Cabet went to London and spent some days in conference with Robert Owen.   As the result of that
conference, the *Populaire* announced that the choice
lay between three localities in the United States
(none of which were specified), and that the final
decision must be deferred until the most thorough
investigation had been made of all such matters as
soil, climate, products, streams, etc.   This sounded
very business-like.   There seems little doubt that
Robert Owen advised him to go to Texas, and
that Cabet was pretty fully determined upon that
State.   Nearly twenty years previous, while Texas
was Mexican territory, Owen had been in negotiation with the Mexican government and had visited
the country with the object of planting colonies, so
that he was familiar with its general character.[1]

---

[1] Robert Owen's negotiations with the Mexican Government, after
the failure of his Indiana project, and his visit to Mexico in the fall
of 1828, form one of the most interesting episodes in Owen's remarkable career.   His negotiations were at first very successful, and his

Texas had now been admitted to the Union and was entering upon an era of prosperity. She was in every way inviting immigration to her vast empire of unoccupied land. Large grants were made to private companies on condition of securing immigrants. One of these was the Peters Company, of Cincinnati; and it was with this company that Cabet arranged for his land. He went through the form of sending a commissioner to examine the the property, but he was already satisfied and sanguine as to his chosen location. In the *Populaire*, Jan. 17, 1848, was the following announcement:

## " C'EST AU TEXAS.

" After having examined all the countries suitable for a grand emigration, we have chosen Texas—the northeastern part—as that which presents the most advantages in respect to health, the temperature of the climate, the fertility of the soil, extent of country, etc. We have already obtained more than a million acres of land along the Red River, a beau-

---

schemes of social reform attracted the Mexican President and particularly fascinated Mr. Poinsett, the American Minister, who used his official influence for the success of the negotiation. Mr. Owen secured the promise of an enormous tract, thousands of square miles in extent, in Texas. ·Later the Mexican Congress refused to confirm the grant, and the affair came to nought. But Owen never forgot the daring project of a communistic commonwealth in Texas, and, naturally enough, twenty years later he put the idea into Cabet's head. Though I have no direct evidence, I cannot doubt that Cabet in choosing Texas was simply acting as heir to Owen's large plan of 1828. For an account of Owen's visit to Mexico, see Sargant's " Robert Owen and His Social Philosophy," London, 1860 (pp. 262–276).

tiful stream, navigable up to our very settlement, and we will be able to extend our territory indefinitely.

" CABET."

It had not been intended to begin emigration until the summer of 1848; but persecutions multiplied. Cabet himself was continually charged by the press with being a swindler who had no real intention of founding a colony, and who was obtaining money under false pretences. These irritating circumstances made haste seem desirable, and on the morning of the 3d of February there were assembled on the wharves at Havre sixty-nine picked men, constituting the "first advance guard." These, Cabet said, were to be followed soon by one thousand or fifteen hundred men, composing the "second advance guard," and some weeks later would begin the general emigration. The scene of emigration was a most impressive one. Cabet and his friends, many relatives of the pioneers, and hundreds of curious spectators, thronged the piers. Before sailing, the sixty-nine entered into a solemn engagement with Cabet, in the form of a series of questions to which they assented one by one. For example, they were asked if they gave their adherence without any mental reservation to the " Social Contract," published in the *Populaire* some four months previous. This social contract was simply a provisional constitution, providing for the organization of a communistic society, arranging for its management while in the early formative stages, and making Cabet the Director-in-chief for the first ten years. Other questions put to the advance guard had reference to their sincere devotion to the communistic cause and their willingness to endure privations for its realization. The whole formed a ceremony well adapted to make an indelible impression on the minds of men leaving their native land under circumstances so romantic and peculiar.

Cabet himself was touched with a sense of the heroism of the spectacle. He wrote in the *Populaire*, that in view of men like the advance guard, he "could not doubt the regeneration of the human race." He believed that the 3d of February, 1848, would be forever known as an epoch-making date. "At length," he writes, "on Thursday, February 3d, at nine o'clock in the morning, there was accomplished one of the grandest acts, we believe, in the history of the human race ;—the advance guard, departing on the ship 'Rome,' has left Havre to enter the ocean and voyage toward Icaria. \* \* \* These courageous Icarians, placed on the stern-deck of the ship, entoned in unison the farewell chant, 'Partons pour Icarie,' to which the spectators responded in a thousand cries of 'au revoir !' \* \* \* May the winds and waves be propitious to you, soldiers of humanity! And we, Icarians, who remain, let us prepare without loss of time to rejoin our friends and brothers ! "

# II.

## COLONIZATION IN TEXAS.

# II.

As the ship " Rome," bearing the sixty-nine pioneers, approached New Orleans on the 27th of March, its passengers heard the booming of artillery. But the salute was not in honor of their arrival. A faster ship had brought word from Paris of the Revolution of February 24th, and the French people of New Orleans were celebrating the downfall of Louis Philippe and the establishment of the Second Republic. If the advance guard had tarried three weeks longer in France, the subsequent history of Icaria would doubtless have been something very different from that which is recounted in the following pages. But it is for us to record what was, not what might have been.

The Revolution of 1848 was the rock on which the great Icarian school split. Part of the society advocated the recall of the advance guard, the abandonment of the emigration scheme, and the concentration of every effort for the success of the new Republic. This party hoped for the gradual transformation of France into an Icaria. But on the other hand, the party led by Cabet maintained that

Icarians had nothing to hope from a government controlled by Lamartine, Ledru-Rollin, and others hostile to the Communistic cause. In reality, Louis Blanc, Blanqui, Cabet, and the extremists were now, as in 1830, the men who had precipitated the revolution ; but, as before, they were unable to control its results. Louis Blanc was the only one of their number who obtained a leading place in the new government, and in accordance with his views a series of reforms were at once instituted, almost precisely in the line of those contained in Cabet's "transitional constitution," described in the "Voyage." The "right to labor" was proclaimed by law, and in a few weeks, more than a hundred thousand men were employed in national workshops. Taxes on salt, and other indirect taxes on the necessaries of life were removed, and direct taxes were almost doubled. The interests of the laboring man were solicitously, ostentatiously regarded in the legislation of the Republic. The length of a day's labor was fixed by law. Wages were made matter of legislation. But the triumph of socialism was brief, the workshops proved a dismal failure, and the reform legislation survived only a few weeks.[1] The whole situation,

---

[1] It is now established beyond controversy that Louis Blanc and his socialistic friends were not responsible either for the founding, the bad management, or the failure of the national workshops. They were doomed to failure from the beginning, because they were deliberately planned by anti-socialists in order to throw discredit on the doctrines and the men represented by Blanc. The usual attribution of these measures to Blanc is therefore erroneous. For a proper state-

however, placed Cabet in a painful dilemma. He decided that he could not wisely abandon the colonization, and the hitherto devoted and harmonious body of Icarians was fatally severed.

On the 3d of June the second advance guard left France, but it was not the corps of 1,000 or 1,500 men that had been promised. It was a resolute band of only nineteen !

Here let us turn to follow the fortunes of the sixty-nine pioneers. On learning in New Orleans that the Republic had been proclaimed in France, the question of immediate return was agitated. This view did not prevail, although three or four men left the party determined to go back.[1] It was ascertained that in order to reach the lands of the Peters Company they must go to Shreveport, Louisiana, on the Red River, by steamboat, and advance thence to their destination by teams. The *Populaire* had stated that the land acquired from Peters was washed by the Red River and would be readily accessible by boat ; but on arriving at Shreveport the advance guard discovered a very momentous geographical discrepancy. Icaria was more than two hundred and fifty miles distant (some thirty miles distant from

---

ment of the case, see Ely's " French and German Socialism " (New York, 1883), pp. 111–113.

[1] One of these seceders was a young fellow, A. Piquenard by name. He afterward rejoined the society. In later years he became the most distinguished architect of the West. Among other public buildings he designed the magnificent State Capitols at Springfield, Illinois, and Des Moines, Iowa. He died several years ago at St. Louis.

the spot where the city of Dallas now flourishes),
and must be reached by a march across a wellnigh
trackless wilderness of plains and hills, prairies and
forests, undrained swamps and unbridged streams,
swollen by the spring rains. Like most emigrants,
these pilgrims were encumbered with much unneces-
sary luggage, and provided with too little ready
money. They spent several days in Shreveport trying in vain to procure wagons and teams for the
conveyance of their goods to Sulphur Prairie. (Sulphur Prairie, be it said, was a farm about a hundred
miles from Shreveport, which Sully, Cabet's commissioner, had bought as an Icarian rendezvous and
base of operations; and at this time Sully himself
was lying sick at Sulphur Prairie.) Finally a portion
of the guard started, with two or three ox-teams and
one wagon. The others remained behind until they
had completed a large temporary shed on the edge
of the village, in which shed they stored their trouble-
some and bulky belongings. A most graphic account
of the weary trudge on foot from Shreveport to
Sulphur Prairie and thence to Icaria was written by
Levi de Rheims on the 2d of June, a very few days
after his arrival on the scene of the "new terrestrial
paradise." This letter, written to relatives and
friends in France, found its way into print, and a
copy of it is among my materials for this sketch.
From the arrival at New Orleans to the arrival at
Icaria, almost two months had elapsed. Strangers

in a strange land, unable to speak English, ignorant of almost every thing which a pioneer should know, their hardships were only exceeded by their fortitude and good cheer. Sickness by the way, the breaking down of their one wagon, the wading of dangerous streams, the insufficient supply of food, sleeping on the damp ground,—the whole situation can hardly be realized by one who has not experienced something of life in a wilderness.

At Sulphur Prairie they found a new cause of anxiety and haste. They had been assured by Cabet and by the *Populaire* that a million acres of land had already been acquired. Here also, as in the case of the geographical situation, they found a painful discrepacny. The acquisition was discovered to be not absolute, but on condition of actual colonization. Each man could secure and hold a half-section (320 acres) by building a house upon it and living therein. This would give free possession. But this offer held good only until July 1st. After that date, land would have to be purchased at one dollar an acre. When July 1st arrived, it was found that their utmost efforts had availed to build thirty-two very small log-cabins. They were, therefore, in possession, not of 1,000,000 acres, but of 10,240. As it was a journey of more than three months from Paris to Icaria, emigrants leaving France later than the month of March could not possibly have arrived in time to secure land under the contract with Peters.

But it remains to relate another sad discrepancy.
The thirty-two half-sections were not contiguous!
The State of Texas had granted to the Peters Company each alternate section (square mile, 640 acres)
of a certain tract of land, on condition that the
company should secure immigration. The company
had in turn granted the Icarians the privilege of
acquiring by actual residence the half of each of its

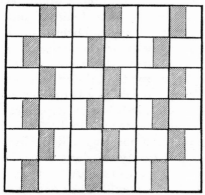

sections, to the extent of a million acres. Cabet's
million acres would therefore have been checkered
over a territory of four millions, and the 10,240
acres were scattered through two townships. The
accompanying diagram represents a single township
(thirty-six sections), the blank sections representing
the land reserved by Texas, the blank half-sections
that reserved by the Peters Company, and the

shaded half-sections showing the disjointed character of the Icarian domain.

It needs no argument to show that a colony intending to live grouped in a village, with a unitary *cuisine* and dining-hall and a coöperative system of agriculture and industry, must have its land in a compact body. The possibility of buying the alternate half-sections from Mr. Peters and the alternate sections from the State of Texas was entirely too remote and uncertain to have been relied upon. In spite of all this disheartening outlook, the pioneers kept pretty good spirits, and set resolutely to work to establish a central headquarters, in anticipation of the large arrivals expected. A log-house fifteen feet wide by twenty-five long was achieved, and three or four long covered sheds. The summer was far advanced, but it was obviously necessary to put in a crop. A plow had been purchased, and they set about "breaking" prairie. But, alas! they knew not how. In turning the matted virgin sod of the prairie for the first time, the Western farmer never sinks his plow-share deeper than two or three inches; but these young French tailors and shoemakers knew nothing about Western farming, and they drove the plow in clear to the beam. It was what is known in Western parlance as a large "breaking plow," and they fastened twenty oxen to it. They broke their plow very promptly, but they never "broke" any Texas prairie. For by this time the middle of

July was past, and man after man succumbed to an intermittent malarial fever, till there was not a well person in the camp. The unaccustomed heat, their arduous and imprudent labors, and their unacclimated condition had subjected them to a terrible scourge. Their physician became sick, then hopelessly insane. Four men soon died of the fever. Another was killed by lightning. Those least sick prepared food and cared for their more helpless comrades.

August was passing away. It was now too late to think of putting in a crop, even if they had been able to do the work. It took letters several months to reach France, and they knew that before word could be received from Texas their own wives and families, as well as many additional Icarians, would have embarked for America. To prepare either the settlement on the Peters lands or the camp at Sulphur Prairie for the winter-quarters of a large body of immigrants was now seen to be practically impossible. In June, the pioneers had been cheerful, and had written home glowing, enthusiastic accounts of the beauty and evident richness of the vast prairies, with their fine streams bordered with heavy timber fringes. But a wild southwestern prairie in the flowery months of May and June seems a much more inviting and hospitable place than under the withering sun and scorching winds of August. The fever had dispirited the Icarians, and the country had become loathsome to them.

They resolved to abandon it. Indeed, to have done otherwise would have been mistaken heroism.

About the middle of September, after a residence of scarcely four months in Texas, the enfeebled Icarians began a straggling retreat to Shreveport. They had produced nothing and had bought many of their supplies from the agent of the Peters Company, whom they now reimbursed by turning over to him their oxen and other articles of equipment. They were far too numerous to march in a body, for the few scattered farm-houses along the three hundred miles between them and Shreveport could not be expected to furnish food for a company numbering several scores of famishing men. The last money in the treasury was divided, and each man, with gun and haversack and six or seven dollars, began the journey. By different routes and in small squads of two, three, or four men, travelling faster or slower as their strength would permit, most of them had reached Shreveport at the end of a month. Four or five had died by the way. Nothing in Icarian annals is more doleful than this retreat of the Texas invalids.

The little squad composing the second advance guard participated in this retreat. They had landed at New Orleans, July 22d, and ten or twelve of them had reached Icaria on August 29th, others remaining sick at Sulphur Prairie. Two or three days after his arrival, Favard, the leader of the second advance guard, had written home to Cabet the following letter:

"ICARIAN COLONY, *Sept.* 2, 1848.
"POOR FATHER :—
"How can I depict to you the situation in which I have found our brothers? Almost all those who survive are sick. Four are dead; the first was Guillot, the second, Collet, who was killed by lightning, the third was Guérin, and the fourth Tangé.

"Those least sick attend to the *cuisine* and the fatigue makes them fall sick again.

"The sun is so hot that if one is exposed to its rays he is almost certain to have the fever. I have not hesitated an instant in favoring the abandonment of the camp—which also seems best to all ; for many have only awaited our arrival in order to have the assistance which would enable them to get away.

"We should not be able to bring the women here by these abominable roads. Wagons could not make more than two or three leagues a day. One finds no villages, but only farm-houses at long intervals, and in none of them have they beds for four persons. One does not even find bread ; for the people of the country do not make bread except in small quantities at the very moment of eating.

"When we started from Shreveport we left there our trunks and mattresses. We loaded our wagons with provisions for our brothers and ourselves. We placed in our haversacks such clothing as was indispensable and a blanket, and thus departed. We slept out of doors during the entire route. We had beautiful weather all the time ; but that did not prevent eight [8 out of 19] of our men from falling sick, and it was necessary to leave them *en route.* Edouard remained with them as nurse.

" I continued on the road with the others, and we arrived here in good health. All our attention is given to those who are most ill, and to preparations for departure. But what is most annoying is that we have incurred a debt of seven or eight thousand francs, and we are embarrassed for the means to liquidate it under the circumstances. If we can arrange with our creditors we will occupy ourselves exclusively with our retreat to Shreveport. We will join in writing you a letter making you acquainted with all our affairs, * * *

" Ever your devoted

" FAVARD."

Cabet received this discouraging letter early in November, but did not think it best to publish it until about the first of December. It does not seem to have occurred to him that he was in any wise responsible for the sad *fiasco.* We read in the *Populaire* in his bright, glowing style a most sympathetic epitome of their hardships,—the story, as he says, " of an ardor, a zeal, a devotion, a courage almost superhuman." " But," he reprovingly suggests, "this was not prudent under a new climate." He proceeds to recount the praises which all their letters have bestowed upon the general features of the country, and he asserts that if they had labored more moderately, had cared for themselves more prudently during the heated term, and had had their baggage and medicines and proper food, "all our hopes would have been realized." He further endeavors to show how the February revolution had greatly contributed to the disaster. It had overthrown Icarian plans in France, destroyed financial resources, prevented the sending of men and money to the aid of the pioneers, and had been in every way paralyzing and distracting. Thus Cabet laid all the blame on the imprudence of the pioneers and the events of the Revolution, and it seems never to have crossed his mind that his own sanguine and immature sort of planning had really been the chief cause of disaster. He concludes this rather unsatisfactory article by saying that if the first and second guards would decide to return from Shreveport to Sulphur Prairie, which, he adds, they were morally certain to do, "*all would yet be saved.*"

"All would yet be saved." Just what Cabet meant by this it is difficult to say. Perhaps it was not quite clear in his own mind. As a practical financier and manager, Cabet's limitations were already becoming conspicuous. By this time the general emigration had begun. In several different vessels as many as four hundred Icarians arrived at New Orleans toward the close of 1848. Last of all Cabet came himself. He embarked from France the 15th of December and arrived in January.

Affairs had gone unfortunately with our politician, littérateur, and philosopher. He had fully believed that his colony would be carried on a tremendous wave of popularity, and had made no provision for possible reverses. The finances of the society were at low ebb. In fact the society had never had any firm financial basis. Before the first advance guard had sailed, the *Populaire* had published a "*Plan Financier*," which is rather a remarkable document. It begins by frankly confessing that Icaria lacks the funds for the proposed emigration, and that their cause would seem hopeless but for the fact that it was based upon grand truths, such as could be relied upon to win universal confidence and sympathy, and open universal purse-strings. The "Plan" proceeds to give five sources whence the necessary capital would be forthcoming. First, the property of the members. At least 600 francs for preliminary expenses would be required of all who joined the emigration. Second, gifts and subscriptions for Icaria. An appeal was made to all classes to aid so beneficent and glorious a movement. Third, loans, which might be contracted with companies, large capitalists, and even with common people in sums as small as 500 francs. These loans would be secured by mortgage on the real estate of the prospective Icaria, which real estate Cabet declared would "augment in value tenfold, fifty-fold and even a hundred-fold." Fourth, it was expected that credit could be obtained for the larger purchases and negotiations. Fifth, "we will establish a bank and issue circulating notes, as is the usage in America for grand enterprises which inspire sympathy and confidence ! "

So ethereal and precarious a scheme may well make us smile ; but we must remember that more experienced men have often embarked in less promising enterprises. The " Plan " read smoothly, had a plausible appearance, and was not subjected to very critical scrutiny by the enthusiastic young *ouvriers*, whose sublime faith in Cabet made them ready to brave any thing at his bidding.

Besides the colonization scheme and its reverses, Cabet must have been at this time greatly occupied with French politics. It was not possible for him to be in France without being a participant in the incessant agitations of the entire year 1848. Those were times when it was literally impossible to tell what a day would bring forth. If Cabet had some political aspiration, some dream of being a Minister or even a President, it was pardonable under the circumstances. We actually find him mentioned during the fall as one of the seven or eight more prominent presidential candidates, Louis Napoleon, Cavaignac, and Lamartine leading in the list. But there was no prospect of his election, and five days before the overwhelming vote in favor of Louis Napoleon was thrown, Cabet left France with declining fortunes behind him and prospects none too brilliant before him.

Early in 1849, then, we find the Icarian pilgrims of seven or eight successive embarkations, and numbering in all about four hundred and eighty souls, reunited with their founder and leader at New Orleans. Their treasury contained somewhere near 86,000 francs—$35 per capita. It is hardly too conservative an estimate to say that people founding a home in an entirely undeveloped country should have sufficient capital to provide for fully two years' sustenance besides all other expenses. If it had been decided to return to Sulphur Prairie, the 86,000 francs, after deducting transportation and other unavoidable expenses, would have furnished support for only a few months. Returning to Texas was therefore out of the question. In the presence of hard realities, the beautiful dream of a million acres on the Red River, with the fine roads and the rapidly rising towns had faded away. For three months the Icarian community controlled no wider premises than those pertaining to two large brick houses on Saint Ferdinand Street, New Orleans. Exploring parties were sent in different directions in search of a new location. Those were weeks of suspense, dampened enthusiasm, and incessant—not always harmonious—discussion. Many wished to return to France. Others desired to secure a more suitable location than Texas, and persevere with the colony.

At length a minority of two hundred withdrew, Cabet allowing them to take $5,000—nearly one third of the precious 86,000 francs. Some of this minority remained in New Orleans, but the larger number returned to France, no more to embark in Utopian enterprises. Some two hundred and eighty souls remained with their leader, heard the reports of the returned explorers, agreed upon a location, and early in March took passage on a Mississippi steamer for their new home.

# III.

## COMMUNITY LIFE AT NAUVOO.

## III.

IF these people had been of a religious mind, they might well have believed that their new home was providentially prepared for them. In 1840 Joseph Smith had brought his Mormon followers from Missouri to Hancock County, Illinois, and had built the town of Nauvoo in a beautiful bend of the Mississippi, and on a magnificent tract of agricultural land. In four or five years the Latter-Day Saints at Nauvoo numbered 15,000, and their prosperity was remarkable. At this time Chicago had only 8,000 people, and Nauvoo was the largest and most flourishing town in the State. But, as in Ohio, and afterward in Missouri, so now in Illinois the active hostility of "Gentile" neighbors was too intense to be withstood. Smith was killed, and the new prophet, Brigham Young, organized the migration to Salt Lake—a migration as absolutely unique and remarkable as any ever recorded. This two years' migration was now practically completed, and Nauvoo was an almost empty town. The Mormons still had large properties there in land and houses, and had left an agent in charge.

Here, then, was the opportunity for the Icarians. Their resources forbade the immediate occupation of the virgin soil on the frontier; but at Nauvoo they could find good houses ready built, and good land that had been brought under cultivation. Best of all, they were not obliged to exhaust their scanty treasury by the purchase of land, for under the circumstances it could be rented at a merely nominal figure. It was indeed well for them that they had thus found a ready-made home, for they were dispirited and homesick. On the boat up the river they had been attacked by the cholera, and had lost twenty of their number. The division at New Orleans had parted many friends. The deaths in Texas and on the Mississippi had left many mourners.

On the 15th of March they landed at Nauvoo. They purchased some houses in the village, rented perhaps 800 acres of land, bought a mill and a distillery, and set their social life in the best order that circumstances would permit. We will not concern ourselves with their doings for the first year or two, while they were fitting themselves to their surroundings, and were at work on the problem of adjusting their actual life to their Icarian theories. We must simply remember that they were average Frenchmen, abundantly endowed with the ordinary traits of human nature, trying sincerely to adopt a more equal, unselfish, altruistic life ; that they were embarking in a difficult enterprise without the advantage either of experience or capital; that they were artisans from French cities founding a community based on agriculture; that they were ignorant of the language, laws, customs, and business methods of the country; and that their leader was rather a patriot, agitator, and theorist than a practical business manager.

In 1854 or 1855, the visitor would have found the colony well established and measurably prosperous. Suppose we imagine ourselves shown through the establishment by the bland and affable Cabet, president of the community. On a tract of some fifteen acres were the principal Icarian buildings, clustered on and about the old " Temple Square " of the Mormons. The Mormons had left unfinished a huge " temple " of dressed white limestone, one hundred and twenty-eight feet long, eighty feet wide, and with walls sixty feet high. A fire in 1848 had destroyed the interior, but the bare walls stood massive and uninjured. Cabet bought the property with the intention of completing the temple and transforming it into a grand Icarian assembly and dining hall, school-rooms, etc. But shortly after the work of restoration had begun, a tornado blew down the north wall, and the building was henceforth utilized only as a stone-quarry whence materials were taken for other structures. The main Icarian building was one hundred and fifty feet by thirty, two stories high, and the first floor was used as the common dining-hall, an assembly room, theatre, etc., while the upper rooms were used as dwellings. A large two-story stone building was erected for educational purposes. Another large stone building, the old Mormon arsenal, was bought and transformed into workshops. For dwelling purposes a forty-room brick house had been purchased of the Mormons and a number of smaller houses were bought, built, or rented. Thus the question of habitations had been fortunately disposed of.

Membership, meanwhile, had doubled, and we find a community numbering upward of five hundred,[1] while as many more had come, tarried awhile, and departed. We find a thousand acres or more of rented land under cultivation. The chief industries are a flouring mill, saw mill and whiskey distillery. Various small workshops, tailoring, shoemaking, blacksmithing, carpentering, and the like supply the needs of the community and are a source of income by taking outside work. Good schools are maintained in which boys and girls are taught separately and taken very young. English, French, mathe-

---

[1] Mr. Nordhoff is in error when he says that Cabet "had at Nauvoo at one time not less than fifteen hundred people." (*Vide* "Communistic Societies of the United States," p. 334.) Membership never reached six hundred at any one time. But members were coming and going continually, and it is not unlikely that as many as fifteen hundred different individuals were at one time or another connected with Icaria between 1849 and 1856.

matics, drawing, history, and geography are taught, but mere cramming is not the object of the school. Careful training in manners and morals, and in Icarian principles and precepts, is work with which the schools are especially charged. The printing-office is a place of great activity. Newspapers are printed in English, French, and German. Icarian school-books are published, treating of the history and doctrine of the community as well as of the common branches of knowledge. Pamphlets, news-papers, and books designed to aid the propaganda in France are industriously produced, and dis-tributed through the agency of the Icarian Bureau at Paris. It is pleasant to find that the community is a model of industry, intelligence, peace and good order, that family life is sacredly regarded, and that the Nauvoo neighbors, whose experience with the Mormons had naturally made them at first suspicious of the new French colonists, have now learned to es-teem them highly. A library of five or six thousand volumes, chiefly standard French works, seems to be much patronized. Though obliged, as they explain, by circumstances to operate a distillery as a leading means of support, we see the Icarians discounte-nancing the use among themselves of alcoholic drinks and also of tobacco. They have not lost their love for public amusement, and a well-trained band discourses good music at the numerous fêtes of the community. Frequent theatrical entertain-

ments, social dances, and lectures are common means
of diversion, and attract many outside visitors. The
style of living is economical, hard labor is a necessity; but it must be admitted by the intelligent
visitor that the Icarian system is enabling these
families to live a less sordid life, one more social,
humane, intellectual, and less grinding, toilsome,
and degrading than that of the average workingman
under the system of individualism and competition.
They are far from the condition of the happy Icarians in the "Voyage," but considering the difficulties they have encountered they must be accredited
with having done reasonably well.

It was from the outset the intention to make Nauvoo only a temporary home ; and as early as 1852
a number of men were sent into southwestern Iowa
to acquire government land, and begin its improvement with the purpose of ultimately removing the
community thither. At the end of the year 1855,
we find that the official inventory of the community's
property, exclusive of that in Iowa, sums up $76,
439.76, from which should be deducted a debt of
$11,633.23, leaving a net valuation of $64,806.53.
In addition to this, the community owned in Iowa
over three thousand (3,115) acres of land with some
crude improvements on the tract. Unless some
serious reverses should overtake them, the Icarians
had now reached the point from which they might
expect rapid material prosperity. Unhappily, the

reverses were already impending. The difficulties were in connection with the government of the society.

In an earlier chapter I have spoken of the impressive scene at Havre when the first advance guard assented to the "Icarian Engagement" and the "Social Contract," promising among other things to accept Cabet as dictator for ten years. These engagements were also taken by the several parties embarking successively during the year 1848, and were renewed at New Orleans and again renewed on arriving in Nauvoo. However, before the community had lived in Nauvoo a year, Cabet resolved to relinquish his absolute authority, and to give his people a constitution. The document was submitted and unanimously adopted in February, 1850. It is so long that a synopsis of its chief provisions must suffice here. It provided for six directors, called a "Committee of Gerance," elected for a year, three being chosen every six months. One of these was to be elected separately as President of the Icarian Community. These six divided among themselves the work of administration as follows: 1st., Presidency and General Superintendence; 2d., General Direction of Finances and Provisions; 3d., Clothing and Lodging; 4th., Education, Health, and Amusements; 5th., Industry and Agriculture; 6th., Secretaryship and Management of the Printing-office. Legislative authority was vested in the

General Assembly, which met every Saturday, and was composed of every male member of the community twenty years old. The Committee of Gerance were responsible to the Assembly. The constitution was subject to revision every second year. Admissions to the community were first provisional; then definitive, by vote of the Assembly, after six months' probation. In case of withdrawal, half of the property brought into the community by the individual was returned to him.

One of Cabet's objects in granting this constitution was the procuring of a charter of incorporation from the Illinois Legislature. The Mormon charter had been revoked by the Legislature during the trouble at Nauvoo, and there had remained a very strong prejudice against chartering peculiar societies. Cabet's constitution contained a great amount of preliminary and general matter explaining the moral and social virtues of the Icarian system, and appealing to the approbation of the average legislator by expressing many of the glittering political maxims of the American Declaration of Independence. Notwithstanding this unexceptionable constitution, the community had some difficulty in getting its charter, the act finally passing by a small majority. Under the new organic law, Cabet was elected President, and was unanimously reëlected from year to year. But on more than one important subject differences of opinion began to appear. Cabet was not always wise, and a number of younger and more practical men found themselves frequently at variance with him. He was now nearly seventy years old, and was perhaps growing more arbitrary and determined in the exercise of power while becoming less capable of exercising it wisely.

The breach was widening imperceptibly, and its extent was not realized by either party until in December, 1855, when Cabet made a proposition for a radical change in the constitution. He proposed the abolition of the governing board of directors, the so-called "Committee of Gerance," and the substitution of a President, to hold office four years, who should have authority to name and to remove at will all the subordinate officers of the community. The constitution distinctly provided for revision every two years, namely, in March, 1853, March, 1855, March, 1857, etc. Cabet's proposition therefore came at an illegal time. It should have been made nearly a year earlier, or more than a year later. Moreover, it violated express provisions of the Illinois charter. Nevertheless, he insisted, and every Icarian took sides,—the majority being against Cabet. The contest grew serious, bitter, and disturbing. A few weeks later, on Feb. 3d (anniversary of the first departure from Havre), came the annual Presidential election. In the meeting of the Assembly on that day Cabet stoutly refused to withdraw his proposition, and hinted darkly at abandoning the society. Thereupon the majority proceeded to choose as President a vigorous young leader of their party, J. B. Gérard by name. Cabet was thoroughly surprised. He consented to withdraw his proposition for a year, and the whole Icarian community met the next day and showed their undiminished personal affection for their old chief by unanimously electing him President, Gérard gladly resigning for that purpose.

Peace seemed to be secured, but hostilities soon opened again. Cabet had most of the Committee of Gerance on his side, and therefore controlled the executive, while his opponents held a steady majority in the Assembly, to which the executive was theoretically subject. Cabet controlled the printing-office and newspaper, and used the press for partisan purposes. Dissension now so threatened the permanence and prosperity of the society that many withdrew from membership. The Assembly appointed an investigating committee who condemned the management of the printing-office. Another committee investigated the affairs of the Icarian Bureau in Paris. This was in the charge of Madame Cabet and other members of the family. It had been a centre of propaganda and information, had secured recruits, and had been the European fiscal agency of the community, negotiating loans and receiving donations. Cabet had made use of it for the distribution among the thousands of Icarians in France of bulletins and circulars which were secretly printed at Nauvoo and were full of denunciations against the actions of the majority. The committee reported that the Bureau was expensive, ill-managed, and hostile to the majority of the community, and recommended its immediate suppression. The recommendation was adopted by the Assembly. Cabet now brought in proposals of separation, his plan being that one party should remain at Nauvoo and the other occupy the Iowa domain. But a party which was in the majority and legally in the right could hardly be expected under the circumstances to cede half the common estate to a disaffected, turbulent, and law-breaking minority. So all hope of amicable separation fell to the ground.

Both parties rushed into print voluminously enough, with memorials, resolutions, pamphlets, polemics, and appeals to the world; but though I have collected a quantity of such materials relating to this bitter little civil war, I must hasten the recital lest the story become tedious. I have already stated that half the Committee of Gerance were elected in February, and half six months later —viz., August 3d. The majority of the Gerance were still Cabetists. The date of the August election arrived, and the anti-Cabet party elected their own candidates, thus at length obtaining preponderant executive influence. Cabet and the minority refused to submit to the election, and the old members of the Gerance would not yield up their offices to the newly elect. Excitement and enmity now reached their climax, and the civil authorities of Nauvoo intervened to prevent probable bloodshed. The new directors were installed by force. The whole Cabet party thereupon ceased to work at their places in shops, fields, and mills. For months the party lines had been drawn everywhere. In the Assembly the opposing factions had occupied opposite sides of the hall; at meals they had taken separate tables; the little children at school had become partisans. Now the majority decided that those who would not work should not eat. The new Gerance assigned every individual his work, and gave notice that those who absented themselves from labor would be cut off from rations after August 13th.

Cabet rented a large building in the village of Nauvoo, and the minority made it their temporary home. Their object now seemed to be to secure the dissolution of the society. By secret letters and messengers Cabet had secured the loyalty of the larger part of those absent on the land in Iowa, and he undertook to effect the abandonment of that estate, which would have entailed severe damage upon the community, since the titles were in Cabet's name, and if the estate had been deserted, the Nauvoo Community would not have the prestige of

" possession," which " is nine points of the law." The alertness of the majority foiled Cabet's scheme in this direction. He also endeavored to bring financial confusion on the community by making damaging statements to its creditors, and representing it as in an unsound condition. He had carried away the records and account books, and as he had always represented the community in its external relations, he was in a situation to injure its credit materially. He further attempted to secure the dissolution of the community by bringing suit in the State courts. This plan was found ineffective, and in a long partisan statement the Cabetists petitioned the Legislature of Illinois to repeal the Act of Incorporation. The Legislature refused to do so by a vote of 55 to 9. In October a committee appointed for that purpose brought into the Assembly a series of formal charges against Cabet which were sustained by unanimous vote, and he was expelled from membership.

The minority had already resolved to spend the winter in St. Louis, where their men, largely tailors and mechanics, could find work pending the adoption of some permanent arrangement. About the 1st of November the minority, comprising one hundred and eighty persons, left Nauvoo. A week later, Nov. 8, 1856, Cabet died suddenly of apoplexy, in St. Louis. He was in his sixty-ninth year. In his threescore years of life in France as a democrat,

revolutionist, and doctrinaire, Cabet had suffered imprisonment, exile, ridicule, slander, persecution by
the officers of church and state; but nothing had
ever so pained and shocked him as his rejection at
Nauvoo.  He had grown old; he had long since
abandoned all idea of preferment and power in
French public life; nothing was left to him but the
colony he had founded.  And he had so identified
himself with its fortunes that he unconsciously mag-
nified his own importance to the community.  It
seemed to him his very own.  Any dissent from his
opinion was treason.  The democratic government
which he had himself granted became an evil thing
in his eyes, because it sometimes obstructed his own
necessary, beneficent, and pre-eminently wise government.  Cabet must not be too severely blamed
for the plots, subterfuges, and machinations he employed in the quarrel.  He was hardly responsible
for his conduct.  He had lost the power to view
Icaria as a thing separate from his own personality;
he was not a part of the community—the community was a part of him.

Cabet was so industriously calumniated and un-
dervalued in France by contemporary writers hostile
to socialism, that the lies have, in part at least,
stuck; and neither his character nor his ability have
been appreciated at their true worth.  He had
faults, more than one of which I have been obliged
already to show.  But he was a better and truer man

than his Parisian detractors. He was ambitious; but more than once he sacrificed office, fortune, and prospects rather than be false to his convictions and his sense of public duty. Disaffected persons who had left the community at New Orleans and returned to France charged him with embezzlement before the French courts and in his absence secured against him a verdict of guilty. Hearing of the matter he journeyed from Nauvoo to Paris to vindicate himself. In the spring of 1852 he triumphantly refuted all charges preferred against him and was formally acquitted by the court.[1]

Cabet's literary work, done chiefly in the intervals of a life busy with other pursuits, was considerable in amount and not devoid of merit. A list of his

---

[1] Professor Richard Owen of New Harmony, Ind., a son of the distinguished English reformer, Robert Owen, furnishes me with two or three pleasant incidents connected with this visit of Cabet's to Europe. It would seem that on his return from France he stopped in England to see his old friend and counsellor, Owen. For, says my informant : " In Part XXI. of Robert Owen's Journal, June 5, 1852, an account is given of the toasts and responses, on May 14th, when celebrating my father's birthday at Anderton's Hotel, Fleet St. My father responded to the first and second toasts, ' The Queen,' ' Robert Owen ' ; the third, ' The distinguished social reformers from abroad,' etc., etc., was responded to by MM. Cabet, Pierre Leroux, Walter Cooper, and Lloyd Jones." As to honors paid Cabet on his arrival in New York, Mr. Owen also says : " I find in my father's periodical (' Robert Owen's Journal,') Part XXV., Sept. 25, 1852, a paragraph copied from the *New York Tribune* of July 9th giving an account of a banquet at the Shakespeare Hotel, N. Y., on July 8th, in honor of M. Cabet, at which M. E. Chevalier [the French economist] proposed his health, and M. Cabet ' responded in an interesting and eloquent speech,' etc. On the next page [of Owen's Journal] is an extract from *The Popular Tribune*, organ of the Icarian community. It is headed : ' Arrival of M. Cabet at Nauvoo.' All this shows the strong interest my father took in the movements of M. Cabet."

writings has never been placed on record. Those
which I shall name in this paragraph have all come
under my notice, and I have heard of no others of
importance. The five-volume "Histoire Populaire
de la Révolution Française de 1789 à 1830," is his
most extensive work. The "Voyage en Icarie"
and the "Vrai Christianisme" have already been
sufficiently described and are without question the
author's best productions. "Douze Lettres d'un
Communiste à un Reformiste sur la Communauté"
(1841–2, pp. 166) was published a year after the
appearance of the "Voyage," in explanation and
defence of its doctrines. The "Refutation du
Dictionnaire Politique (articles Babouvisme, Communauté, Association, Propriété) et de la Revue des
Deux Mondes (sur le Communisme)," the character
of which is sufficiently obvious from the title, appeared in the fall of 1842. In the previous year
also he had published an important pamphlet de-
fending marriage and the institution of the family,
and entitled "Réfutation de l''Humanitaire' (de-
mandant l'abolition du mariage et de la famille)."
Deploring the hostility between French communistic sects and journals, he wrote in 1845 a little book
of fifty-six pages, "Le Salut est dans l'Union ; la Concurrence est la Ruine." "Les Masques Arrachés"
(1845, pp. 144) is a controversial defence of communism. Cabet took advantage of his visit to
France to publish in 1852 a "Lettre du Citoyen

Cabet a l'Archevêque de Paris en Réponse à son Mandement du 8 Juin, 1851." The Archbishop had issued a mandate severely condemning communism, and Cabet in a pamphlet of forty-seven pages refers him to the communistic practices of the Apostles and the early Church, cites the opinions of the Church fathers, etc. "Procés et Acquittement du Citoyen Cabet Accusé d'Escroquerie pour l'Emigration Icarienne" is a volume of two hundred and forty pages, in which are compiled the evidence, correspondence, addresses, etc., relating to Cabet's trial for embezzlement. I have seen no copies of the "Icarian Almanac," published from 1843 to 1847, —a work which seems to have played an important part in the propaganda. The "Realization du Communisme" (1847) is a volume filled with extracts from the *Populaire* respecting the proposed emigration. To this list of writings might be added a very large number of pamphlets, some published in France and some at Nauvoo.

# IV.

## THE CHELTENHAM EPISODE.

# IV.

THE Icarians, one hundred and eighty in number, who had accompanied Cabet in his retreat from Nauvoo to St. Louis, had relied in every thing upon their leader; and his death was a terrible blow to them. A romantic young German, Fritz Bauer, committed suicide in his grief, and the whole group were hardly less disconsolate. But, the first moment of stupor past, they took courage. They had, on October 13, 1856, before leaving Nauvoo, taken an engagement to remain faithful to Icaria and its founder; and they now resolved unanimously that the best mode of honoring the memory of their departed leader and of testifying to their faith in his principles consisted in remaining united and continuing his work.

They installed themselves as well as they could in St. Louis, intending as soon as possible to acquire a tract of land somewhere further west for a permanent home. Meanwhile the men, who were nearly all tailors, shoemakers, or mechanics of some description, found work in the city. Explorers were sent in various directions to discover the promised land, but nothing was found which met all the conditions requisite. In May, 1858, the search was given up and an estate called Cheltenham, lying six miles west of St. Louis, was purchased.

This place afforded some advantages as a domicile for the community. It was near the city, and the men could continue to work at their trades. It possessed a large stone house capacious enough to lodge the greater portion of the colony, besides six log-houses. Unfortunately there were only twenty-eight acres of land, and the price paid was very large—$25,000. Further, the location was unhealthy, and the intermittent fever was as regular in its semi-annual visits as the appearance of spring-time and fall. It was much better, however, than remaining in St. Louis, crowded into several scattered houses; and it was with elation that the new home was entered on May 8, 1858.

During the sojourn in the city a few families had withdrawn, and at the time of removal the membership was not above one hundred and fifty. This is as large a number as was ever reached at Cheltenham; for though accessions from France were made almost continually, the withdrawals were quite as numerous and constant. At once upon their removal the Icarians set about perfecting their social and industrial organization. They established workshops of tailors, joiners, wheel-wrights, blacksmiths, painters, shoemakers, etc. All these shops, of course, did work for outsiders, in addition to supplying the Icarians themselves, and were sufficiently prosperous to furnish a comfortable support for the establishment as well as to meet the first payments on the property as they became due.

The Cheltenham community was exceedingly active in propaganda. It had many correspondents, it published a journal and a number of books, and it maintained at Paris the Bureau which the Nauvoo majority had so bitterly condemned for its partisanship. The Bureau printed and circulated many *brochures* throughout France. Cabet's name and the efforts of the bureau gave the Cheltenham branch a *prestige* which the Nauvoo brethren lacked, and the former was recognized in France as the only original and genuine Icarian community. Thus the men and money sent to reinforce the Icarian cause were all diverted to St. Louis, and the Nauvoo people strove in vain to get a hearing in France. Many recruits were forwarded through the activity of the Bureau, and a loan opened in Paris, in 1857, produced the considerable sum of 50,000 francs among Icarian disciples.

All now went prosperously; hope and enthusiasm reigned in Cheltenham. Schools were opened for the boys and girls, and a " salle d'asile "—a sort of kindergarten—for the smallest children. The band of music and the theatre, so dear to the French heart, were not wanting. In 1858 the so-called

"Cours Icarien" was inaugurated. This was a Sunday-afternoon assembly which contributed much to the intellectual and moral well-being of the community. The programme usually consisted of select readings from the works of Cabet and other authors, recitations by the school-children, and discourses on various subjects by the more accomplished members of the community. It was a school for mutual improvement in things moral and mental. Progress was also making in the payment of the debt on the property; and thus the material as well as the moral situation was satisfactory. Still a few years of courage, union, and perseverance, and the community of Cheltenham would be in condition to undertake, with good guaranties of success, its removal to some ampler and more suitable domain.

But this was never to be realized. In May, 1859, the community entered upon a discussion of the social and political constitution. Two radically distinct parties were developed. The majority adhered faithfully to the later ideas entertained by Cabet, and believed in investing very large if not absolutely dictatorial authority in some chosen leader,—some "*gerant unique*" directing the moral and material affairs of the community. The minority, however, were unalterably opposed to so undemocratic a system of government. Difference of opinion degenerated into party strife; and the vanquished minority, numbering forty-two persons, left the community.

This proved the death-blow to Cheltenham. From the date of this withdrawal the community declined in every way. Many of the most intelligent members, many of the most skilful craftsmen, were among those who withdrew, and the loss was irreparable. The depleted society struggled heroically for five years longer in spite of a series of untoward events which seemed to be in conspiracy to crush it down ; and in 1864 there remained only eight " citoyens," seven " citoyennes," and some children. Thus had the number been reduced to a residue of the bravest and most persistent spirits.

The mortgagee was pressing for payment and threatening to take the property. Funds were exhausted, and there were no available sources of revenue. The propaganda had ceased, and no more aid came from France. A last effort was still made. Two members were sent to Nebraska to find an eligible location on the public lands. But on their return the *morale* was so weakened, and the funds requisite to accomplish the removal were so completely lacking, that the undertaking had to be abandoned.

It was a moment of profound sorrow for these eight families when they met for the last time in the capacity of an Icarian Assembly, to hear the President, A. Sauva,[1] formally announce the disso-

---

[1] For the materials from which this chapter is prepared, I am entirely indebted to Mr. Sauva, who at my request wrote me out, in

lution of the community. There were few words
and many tears. In March, 1864, Sauva bestowed
the keys upon the mortgagee, and the last Icarian
left Cheltenham.

---

French, a little sketch of Cheltenham upon which the chapter is
based. In several places I have rendered into English Mr. Sauva's
own expressions.

# V.

## PIONEER LIFE IN IOWA.

# V

IT need scarcely be said that the community at Nauvoo had been greatly weakened by the split. Much of the movable property, all of the account books, a large portion of the library, had been carried off by the seceders. The titles to the real estate, both in Nauvoo and in Iowa, were in Cabet's name, and long, tedious suits were required in order to give the community perfect legal title to its own premises. The whole system of industry had been deranged. Crops had failed. Debts had greatly increased. The St. Louis party, claiming as we have already shown, to be the real Icarians and maintaining the old Bureau in Paris, had so industriously circulated their version of the story in France, that the Nauvoo majority were there regarded by their still numerous Icarian fellow-disciples as base ingrates who had overturned the society for selfish ends, driven away their noble benefactor Cabet, broken his heart, and caused his death by their brutal treatment. Letters of explanation sent from Nauvoo to France were returned unanswered. No more funds or recruits came to

Nauvoo. However, the community pursued an active, resolute course. Gérard was made President, and Marchand, a young man especially qualified for the position, was made Secretary and placed in charge of the printing-office. The *Revue Icarienne* was reëstablished and it most ably defended the conduct of the majority in the recent strife.

On the first of January, 1857, the community found itself with two hundred and thirty-nine members, eighteen of whom were absent doing pioneer work on the estate in Iowa. By the official inventory of the same date, the assets of the community (exclusive of the Iowa property) had shrunk to a little less than $60,000, while the debt had grown to nearly $19,000. In Iowa they owned 3,115 acres of land, of which 273 were under cultivation and about 1,000 were woodland. Several log-houses had been built, and live stock and farming utensils to the value of several thousand dollars had been accumulated.

Four or five years later, in the flush times, such a financial showing would not have been discouraging. But it must be remembered that this was at the beginning of the year 1857. The great panic and business depression of that year could not be weathered by the community. Their industries were no longer a source of profit ; creditors pressed their claims ; Nauvoo property was dead, and could not be made to realize any thing like the inventoried valuation. As to the land in Iowa, the soil of almost the entire State lay wild and uninhabited, and there was no demand for so remote a track as that owned by Icaria. To crown the difficulty Cabet's heirs held the title-deeds and would not yield them up.

In this predicament it was decided that the community should remove to Iowa, and that its property should be placed in the hands of assignees for the benefit of the creditors. Mr. Gérard, the President, and another member withdrew from the society temporarily in order to be qualified to act as assignees. These, with enough members to constitute a board of directors, in order to do business legally under their charter, remained at Nauvoo till the courts had satisfactorily adjusted the titles in Illinois and Iowa, the Nauvoo property had all been sold, and the creditors had all been honorably arranged with. This required more than two years, and it was not until the fall of 1860 that Nauvoo was finally abandoned as the legal headquarters of Icaria. In September of the same year a new charter was procured under the laws of Iowa.[1]

---

[1] Section 3 of the Illinois charter of 1851 read: "The business of said company shall be manufacturing, milling, all kinds of mechanical business, and agriculture." But in Iowa it was illegal for the Legislature to grant special charters to corporations. General laws of the State provided for the formation of banking and other business corporations. These general laws, however, evidently did not contemplate the incorporation of a community; and their provisions were in several respects unsuitable. For the benefit of the Icarians the Legislature was prevailed upon in the spring of 1860 to

In these years of removal and non-production the
society reached a most unenviable financial condition. It retained the Iowa land, but subject to a
mortgage for a large amount. This debt drew ten
per cent. interest, and as the community was unable
to meet the interest payments, the debt was com-
pounding at a fearful rate. Moreover, membership
had become rapidly reduced by withdrawals after
the assignment in 1857.

The Icarian land lay in Adams County, in the
southwestern part of Iowa, about thirty miles north
of the Missouri State line, and about sixty miles
east of the Missouri River. It is upon a great
highway of travel, the main line of the Chicago,
Burlington, and Quincy Railroad passing across the
tract. Four miles to the west lies the prosperous
town of Corning, and twenty miles eastward is the
city of Creston. But, twenty-five years ago, the
railroad was not built, nor was there a house where

---

enact an additional section to the general law of corporations. This
section read as follows : "Corporations for agricultural and horti-
cultural purposes, and cemetery associations may be formed to endure
any length of time that may be provided by the articles of incorporation thereof : *Provided*, such corporation shall not own to exceed
nine sections [5,760 acres] of land, and the improvements and necessary personal property for the management thereof : *and provided
further* that the articles of incorporation shall provide a mode by
which any member thereof may, at any time withdraw from such
incorporation, and also the mode of determining the amount to be
received by such member upon withdrawal ; and also for the
payment thereof to such members subject only to the rights
of the creditors of such incorporation." Under this Iowa law,
therefore, which came into effect July 4, 1860, the Icarians in September following took out a charter as an agricultural society.
Many years later this became a matter of vital consequence.

the towns stand. Where the traveller now finds
rich farms and clustering villages, there then
stretched the virgin prairie. In 1857 there was
not a squatter along the trail for forty miles east of
Icaria. It was indeed a new country. Cabet seems
to have believed that it was necessary for his colony
to begin its life in the greatest possible seclusion.
He wished its members to be free from the influences and attractions of the outside world, and to
be thrown in on themselves as entirely as possible
during the early years of the experiment. It was
with some such thought as this that he chose first
Texas and then southwestern Iowa for a location.
Perhaps, if his community could have grown, as he
had anticipated, into a very populous and diversified
society, it might have found itself able to maintain
a prosperous existence independent of the outside
world, as the Mormons proved themselves able to
do in Utah. And in that case Cabet's choice of a
remote location would doubtless have been well
advised. But a small community, a mere handful
of people, especially people like our French Icarians,
accustomed to a highly complex life in an old and
populous country, can not cut themselves loose from
the great world without peculiar hardships. They
would have done better to remain at Nauvoo, if
possible, or at least to have sought a less remote
locality.

Land under such circumstances has no value, except a speculative or anticipatory one. It is, in the economic phrase, a "free natural agent." It produces sustenance for the tiller, but it has not begun to yield rent, and therefore it gives no surplus to apply toward the purchase price. The present homestead law, which makes wild lands free to actual settlers, is simply just and reasonable on economic principles, and the old law, under which settlers like our Icarian friends were obliged to pay $1.25 per acre, was a hardship. But, if the actual settler on remote lands can not afford to pay any purchase money, much less can he bear an additional weight of mortgages on his land. It is simply a foregone conclusion that he will forfeit his land to the speculative holder, who can afford to await the time when the growth of population and new facilities for transportation will give the land market value. What if the Icarians had lived so frugally that two thirds of their crop would have been net surplus. There was no accessible market for surplus farm products.[1] Such was their situa-

---

[1] The annals of the Western States are full of curious instances of this kind. Within ten years quantities of corn have been burned as fuel· in parts of Missouri and Nebraska; less because of a fuel famine than from want of a market for grain. Being "land poor" is a frequent expression in the West. Thousands of men have committed the mistake of buying lands on credit at what seemed merely nominal prices, but have ruined themselves and forfeited the lands because they had not sufficient capital to hold valueless land until circumstances gave it value. In 1876, in Dakota, the writer found a solitary farmer who had established himself on the shore of a beautiful little lake. The rich shocks of harvested wheat dotted broad acres, and the maize was maturing in his fields. In his granaries were thousands

tion when they settled in Iowa on land which had no actual market value, and yet was mortgaged for three or four dollars an acre, on which ten per cent. annual interest was to be paid. Of course, they paid no interest. The small amount of products which they were able to transport eastward to a market scarcely sufficed to procure clothing, salt, and the most absolute necessaries. The story of their privations and hardships in those days can not be written. It is a story which testifies to their high faith in the principle of communism, and to their personal courage and devotion. The group of small log-huts in which they spent those days remains as a suggestive reminder of pioneer privations.

In 1863 the debt had grown to $15,500. The war of the rebellion, which was the destruction of Cheltenham, was the salvation of the Iowa Icaria. Agricultural products rose to fabulous prices. The Icarians had acquired a flock of sheep; and wool had the double advantage of being readily transportable and of selling at an enormous figure. They improved this favorable juncture and made a settlement with their creditor by allowing him to take two thousand acres

of bushels of fine wheat, stored up from the crops of two or three preceding years. It was a beautiful sight, this flourishing farm in a wide uninhabited region ; but the clear grain was almost as valueless as the chaff. It could not be drawn 150 miles to the nearest railroad market over almost impassable wagon roads with any profit. To-day, however, a prosperous "city" has grown up close by, two or three railroads are accessible, any possible amount of farm surplus commands high prices, and the formerly valueless land now has real and high value.

of their land at five dollars an acre.    For the remaining $5,500 of the debt they succeeded in procuring the money.    It was a fortunate deliverance.

They were left with only a little more than eleven hundred acres of land ; but it was all they needed, for their number was now reduced (1863) to only thirty-five, including men, women, and children.    The withdrawal of members in those years of hardship can not in all cases be attributed to selfish motives or an unwillingness to share privation.    Members had to be fed, clothed, and sheltered ; and to a community unable even to pay interest on its debt, membership may be a cause of added expense rather than a source of advantage and profit.

For the ensuing twelve or thirteen years, life was any thing but ideal and poetic in Icaria, and we need not dwell at length upon its external features. There were few events to break the monotony of secluded farm life.    These were years of patient, self-sacrificing struggle, devoted to the one object of securing a solid material basis for the happy Icaria of the future.    With this end in view these " soldiers of humanity " shrank from no privation.    Little by little they bought back portions of their land. Through their domain ran a stream known as the Nodaway River, overlooking which, on the bluffy upland half a mile away, was their cluster of a score or more of diminutive log dwellings grouped about a larger log structure which was used as common dining-hall and assembly room. On the river they built a grist- and saw-mill, which was patronized by the neighbors, and was the source of a small net income. Their industry, intelligence, and upright conduct gained the favor of all the surrounding country. Now and then an old Icarian family would return ; and by the end of the year 1868, they were able to report a membership of sixty, a domain of over seventeen hundred acres, fairly well stocked with horses, cattle, and sheep, their mills paid for, and their entire indebtedness lifted. Three years later we find the domain increased by two hundred more acres, steam introduced in the mills, a personnel of seventy members, a new framed central hall, sixty feet long and two stories high, carpenter, blacksmith, wagon and shoe shops in operation, and railroad connections with Eastern markets furnished by the completion of the Burlington and Missouri River (now the Chicago, Burlington, and Quincy) Railroad. Such are the meagre annals, for a dozen years, of these disillusioned pioneers, who had hoped that by this time their brilliant demonstration and realization of a beautiful idea would have converted all civilized nations and transformed the face of the earth. Verily, the world had even forgotten their existence.

Doubtless their care and toil for the means made them sometimes forget the end. It would have been strange had it been otherwise. When men and women have spent the best quarter-century of their lives drudging for the bare means of subsistence and haunted by the spectre of debt, even if they do not grow sordid and hard, they tend to become cautious and conservative ; the generous enthusiasms and glowing ideals of youth are toned down and tempered by stern experience. The amenities of life had a poor chance in those miserably built, cramped log-huts, which were not half as large as the average one-room log-house of the American backwoodsman. But even in this condition the Icarians favorably impressed visitors, as the following extracts from letters will show. An intelligent gentleman who visited Icaria in 1869 wrote that he found in the "log-shanties" "a degree of cultivation, courtesy, and kindness not often so generally found among the same number of persons." The same writer continues : "The Icarian community is a success. The best of feeling appears to prevail among them, and we could but feel elated that *here* at least was a demonstration of successful communism. We wish them that good success in the future to which their self-denial and perseverance so richly entitle them." [1] In 1871, another visitor wrote as follows : "The most surprising thing there was the presence of so many intelligent persons content to live in such a squalid way. The kind, hospitable, and tolerant spirit of the association was perfectly fascinating,

---

[1] Letter from Dr. Briggs, in *The Communist*, 1869.

and almost gilded the quasi hog-pasture in which
they live. I thought I perceived in the young people
a goodness and intelligence which will in another
dozen years revolutionize their mode of living and
doing business, and make their society a power in
the land. Indeed, I think there is more vitality and
virtue and hope for humanity at Icaria than in any
other association." [1]

About this time the finances of the community
began to justify the building of better habitations,
and as these were gradually erected (arranged in the
form of a quadrangle enclosing the larger hall), the
old log-huts were one by one abandoned. As Dr.
Gaskin had predicted, the new generation began to
exert a strong influence in the direction of improvements and "progress." Flowers and shade trees
began to be cultivated, and the village took on a
better appearance. Mr. William Alfred Hinds visited
Icaria in the summer of 1876, and the following extracts from a letter which he sent to the *American
Socialist* give a true and graphic picture of life in
the community at that time :

"A dozen small white cottages arranged on the sides
of a parallelogram ; a large central building containing a
unitary kitchen and a common dining-hall, which is also
used as an assembly room and for community amusements, including an occasional dance or theatrical presen-

---

[1] Private letter of J. W. Gaskin, of Chicago, printed in *The Communist*, 1871. Mr. Gaskin some years later proved the sincerity of
this opinion by joining the community.

tation ;　a unitary bake-room and laundry near at hand ;
numerous log-cabins, also within easy reach of the central
building—forcible reminders of the early poverty and
hardships of this people ;　a small dairy-house near the
thatched stable to the south ;　barns for the horses and
sheep to the north : all these buildings on the bluff rising
from the valley of the Nodaway River, and surrounded
by the community domain of over two thousand acres of
fertile land, of which seven hundred have been cultivated, and including, with some timber land, extensive
meadows and pastures, over which range 600 sheep
and 140 head of cattle—the cultivated part having the
present season 5 acres of potatoes, 5 acres of sorghum,
100 of wheat, 250 of corn, one and a half of straw-
berries, besides vineyards, orchards, etc.: behold the
present external aspects of Icaria.

"At the sound of the bell all direct their footsteps to
the central building ;　and should you enter at meal-time
you would see the entire community, now numbering
seventy-five, seated at the oblong and circular tables, as
lively and sociable as French people know how to be.
Over the entrance door you would notice in large letters
the word 'Equality,' and directly opposite the word
'Liberty,' and at one end of the room the suggestive
'1776–1876.'　You would notice also that upon the table
there is an abundance of substantial food, but that every
thing is plain.

"Should you enter the same building at evening you
might find most of the family assembled, some to converse, some to sing their songs of equality and fraternity.
Or should you call on a Sunday afternoon, as was my

good fortune, you might hear selections from the writings of their great apostle, Étienne Cabet, or recitals by the young, or songs, perchance, which would stir your socialistic enthusiasm.   One of these I heard had this refrain :

> ' Travailleurs de la grande cause,
>    Soyons fiers de notre destin ;
> L'egoiste seul se repose,
>    Travaillons pour le genre humain.'

"A recital by a maiden of fifteen was very effective. She put great expression into the words :

> ' Mes frères, il est temps que les haines s'oublient ;
> Que sous un seul drapeau les peuples se rallient ;
> Le chemin du salut va pour nous s'aplanir.
> La grande liberté que l'Humanité rêve,
> Comme un nouveau soleil, radieuse, se leve
>    Sur l'horizon de l'avenir.'

"It is indeed time that hatreds were forgotten and that all people rallied under a single flag.   Shall that flag be Communism ?   The Icarians will enthusiastically answer 'yes' ;  and yet should one inquire whether all hatreds are forgotten in Icaria itself, would the reply be also 'yes' ?" [1]

This last question of Mr. Hinds' was a peculiarly significant one as we shall proceed to show.

---

[1] This letter is quoted by Mr. Hinds in his "American Communities," pp. 67–69.

# VI.

## THE SONS VERSUS THE FATHERS.

# VI.

## THE SONS VERSUS THE FATHERS.

OUTWARDLY Icaria was in a promising state. Its
assets were now equal to about $60,000 dollars, its
membership was increasing, some of the convenien-
ces and a few of the luxuries of life were finding
admittance ; the lads had grown up to be good
farmers; the library was freely used, and French
and American periodicals were eagerly perused by
bright minds.   A generation had now passed since
the great socialistic movement which had stirred
generous souls in every country, which had given
birth to so many enterprises besides Icaria, and
which reached its climax in the eventful year of '48.
And now a new tidal wave of socialism was sweeping Europe and America.   It did not fail to reach
Icaria; and the community was quickened with a
new sense of its moral mission.   The young people
felt a thrill of that grand enthusiasm for humanity
which in '48 had transformed peasants and artizans
into heroes and philosophers.   And so, with a solid,
though moderate, material prosperity, with a hard-
earned knowledge of the practical things of life, and
yet with a high consciousness of a moral mission

which lifted them above that sordidness and mental sloth to which otherwise their mode of life must have degraded them,—with these conditions existing, what stood in the way of a proud and brilliant future for Icaria ?

Alas, the Icarians were again to demonstrate the exceeding difficulty of maintaining harmony in a community based upon the principle of acquiescence in the will of the majority. Party spirit had broken up the great Icarian school in France ; it had divided the colony at New Orleans ; it had violently rent the society at Nauvoo ; it had precipitated the fall of Cheltenham. For some years the elements of a new tragedy had been silently brewing. A writer on American communities has well observed : " It is obvious that the process of transferring the interests of a community from one generation to another, which always has to be done sooner or later, will be at least a painful one. The highest wisdom is needed to make this transfer, and not mar the harmony of the society." The process may be a very gradual one, yet it necessarily involves a more or less serious crisis. The thoughts and manners and maxims of the fathers are not as those of the sons.

In the Icarian contest, which we must now briefly describe, neither party was wholly right nor wholly wrong. As for motives of conduct, it must be assumed that each party felt itself justified. The

party of the old people, who were in the voting
majority, and whom we may call the Constitutional
party, were undoubtedly more nearly right according to the tenets and written law of Icarianism; but
perhaps they may have been too rigid and too little
conciliatory. The party of the young people, whom
we may term the Revolutionary party, were chafing
for change, expansion, progress, and to them the
party of the majority seemed retrogressive and
dead to the cause of humanity. It is not worth
while to trace in detail the growth of these parties,
nor the points at issue between them. Such
breaches tend to widen constantly. The younger
party desired changes in the business management,
and improvements in the method of agriculture.
They wished the franchise given to women,—only
males above twenty years being voters. Perhaps
they were the more anxious for the emancipation of
the sex because it would have changed the voting
majority in assembly to their side. They were for
admission of many new members and for the introduction of a varied industry which would provide
work and maintenance for a much larger number
than could be supported or employed by ordinary
agriculture. The older party were unwilling to try
any rash or doubtful experiments, and their long
experience had made them cautious and circumspect
in admitting strangers.

The younger party were eager for " propaganda."

They had been fired by the events of '71 in Paris, and felt strongly with the new Communism of France, the Social Democracy of Germany, and the Nihilism of Russia. The new ideas were taking sudden and rank growth in America. Socialistic labor parties and socialistic newspapers were springing up in every city, and the movement was rapidly taking shape which was soon to culminate in the rash and unfortunate riots of 1877. In the West the Greenback party, honest and earnest in its rank and file, though misguided by fallacious doctrines and in some cases by false leaders, was proclaiming a form of socialism. The business depression that had followed the panic of 1873, and which kept thousands of workingmen idle, contributed above all else to the menacing form assumed by social agitation. With these new views, and with the anarchical spirit of the new agitation, whether in Europe or in America, the older party of Icarians had little sympathy. In its very essence the Icarian doctrine was one of peace and good-will. Its mission was constructive or nothing. Its work was to teach the world the philosophy of a better social system, and to demonstrate the practicability of that philosophy. It proposed a peaceful and gradual evolution of existing society into the society of the future; and violent subversions would only hinder progress. Such were the opinions of the older party.

I would not affirm that this difference of sympathy was sufficiently defined to form a very distinct issue between the two parties in Icaria, but it certainly contributed, consciously or unconsciously, to widen the breach. The young party wished to fall in line with the large movements outside, to wage a more vigorous propaganda, to make Icaria an asylum for communists. Distrust grew rapidly between the parties. The old people regarded every proposition to admit a new member as a wily move of the minority to gain a vote in the assembly. The following résumé of the situation is from the pen of a versatile young Parisian communist who came at this stormy moment to join Icaria, and who afterward became prominently identified with the party of the young people. The reader should bear in mind that this account, written several years after the events it describes, is entirely from the standpoint of the young party :

"Icaria was also to furnish proof that all things are born of suffering, and that progress is but the prize of brave effort, and of the discussion, the struggle, and distress which accompany it.

"For a long time isolation, privations, an absorbing labor, perhaps also the effects of age, had totally effaced in the eyes of the Icarians the moral mission of Icaria. Very little cared they for its socialistic character, or desired to yield to the consequences of its legitimate destiny. The age of generous illusions was past, the desire

for improvements extinguished ; internal progress no
longer possessed charms for them.   It is not always ego-
tism which makes one a conservative !   The recollection
of an unfortunate past, while inspiring exaggerated fears
for the future, also forces people into inaction or immo-
bility.

"Meanwhile a new generation came upon the stage.
Some old Icarians, in whom the fire of the cause of
humanity still smouldered under the ashes of years,
aided by communistic visitors who were attracted to
Icaria by its ancient renown, communicated to the youth
of the community the heat of their convictions and the
light of their counsels.   Nevertheless, as it is with the
earth on which seed vainly falls, some of the young
people remained insensible to this kind of magnetism.
But, in general, the sons grew rapidly in the love of
progress, and were not slow to manifest the impatience
and discontent which were produced in them by the
resistance, unconsciously systematic, opposed by their
predecessors to every innovation.

"This divergence of views soon created in the heart of
the Assembly a distinction of groups.   The law of affinity
is irresistible !   The members yielded to its power, and
formed parties, one to defend the progressive movement,
the other to oppose it and favor inertia.

"The struggle was at first pacific and quite fraternal.
But soon came the bad habit of mingling personalities in
the controversy.   The friction of irascible characters and
an old leaven of antipathy, brought from Nauvoo and
revived in the heat of the combat, very quickly substi-
tuted absolute incompatibility for the comparative homo-
geneity which had previously existed.

" Two opposing parties encamped face to face. One
was that of the young Icarians, including some aged
people ; the other that of the old Icarians, including
some young people. There were the Progressives and
the Non-Progressives.

" As with all parties, those of Icaria sought recruits—
with this difference, however, between them, that while
the old party endeavored to increase their numbers from
within, the young party, faithful to the principle of admission, especially sought to increase their strength by
new members. Nevertheless, by the law of admission,
the first party possessed the 'open sesame !' of the doors
of Icaria, and it was only with all the fears, all the
anxieties of conservatism that they consented to pro-
nounce the magic words.

" The necessity of gaining the ascendancy became for
each party more and more urgent. Menaces of ostracism
had been lanced by the majority of the old party against
the minority of the young people, and the latter, while
conscious of the advantage it would probably gain by the
admission of new members, was anxious, in its turn,
about the future attitude of the candidates. It was
necessary that these should offer to both parties the
hope of a future support in order to overcome all resistance to their admission.

" The logic of parties is to continually widen the gulf
which separates them. Sentiment may deny this ; reason
does not. Compromises may intervene ; they will never
unite the incompatible. The skepticism which new ideas
profess toward old ways and old notions is at first an
obstacle to this.

" Subject to this rule, the Icarians were so separated at this point that each party foresaw the imminent rupture of the material bond which still held the two groups together.

" This was in the spring of 1876.

" On the 17th of April of the same year, the minority read in the Assembly a document in which it protested against the retrogressive acts of the majority, reproached them for the lack of regard for the rights and opinions of women, their hostility to propagandism, their persecution of the progressives, etc. It affirmed its devotion to the cause, and its purpose to pursue its ideal at all cost, and to this end signified its wish to be separated from the majority, amicably if possible, by legal means if necessary. The majority refused to consider such an unusual demand.

" Meanwhile, four Internationalists had made application for admission to Icaria. Animated by the fears we have mentioned, each party considered it to be its duty to plead its cause in advance before these prospective members. The majority wrote to them : ' Our enemies desire a separation, that they may then divide the property among themselves.' The minority sent its reasons for demanding a separation.

" Thus forewarned, the candidates left New York, in spite of a dispatch from the majority which told them to postpone their coming. On their arrival each party described to them the situation in its own manner. But it is in supreme moments that one trusts to chance. Either from confidence in the result, or because they were willing to risk every thing, the two parties united in admitting the new-comers after only fifteen days of novitiation."

One of these new-comers was Émile Peron himself, the author of the paragraphs quoted above, a young man who had come to New York after the downfall of the Paris Commune. Another was A. Sauva, who years before had come from France to join the Cheltenham Icarians at St. Louis, and had supported that unfortunate enterprise to the very last. He had then served in the Union army, and afterward had returned to France. He was a prominent member of the great organization of the International, and helped to make French history at Paris in 1871. Both were men of marked ability. The new-comers bent their energy to a restoration of harmony, and apparently with gratifying success. It was during this lull that Mr. Hinds made his visit to Icaria and wrote the letter to the *American Socialist* quoted in the preceding chapter.

The annual election, which came on the 3d of February, 1877, resulted most encouragingly. The directors of the two departments of Industry and Agriculture, those most susceptible of improvements such as had been clamored for, were chosen from the young party. With excellent taste the Presidency for the year was confided to Sauva, who had not identified himself with either faction, but had been a peace-maker. This election seemed to indicate a genuine spirit of concession on all sides, and a disposition to sink party differences for the good of the whole which promised well for the community.

But Sauva did not find his administration a bed of roses. It soon became evident that the leaders of the young party were wholly disaffected, and were only waiting for an occasion to insist again upon separation. Although three or four more "men of '71"—and certainly men of "progressive" views—were soon admitted, the young party were not satisfied ; and the refusal of the majority to admit a young candidate whom the minority especially favored, brought to the surface again all the old animosity. Another point of controversy must be mentioned ; not so much because of its intrinsic importance, as because it illustrates a phase of community life.

This was no less a matter than that of " *les petits jardins* "—the little gardens. Prior to 1870, while the families of the community still lived in the log-huts, the privilege had been granted each family of using a narrow strip of ground surrounding the house for a flower-garden, or for cultivation in any way that seemed good to the occupants of the house, in their hours of leisure. These poor pioneers, with their Gallic love of flowers and of gardening, found genuine satisfaction in their bits of ground ; and here a vine, there an apple-tree, a tobacco-plant, or a fragrant bunch of garlic, were added to the original flower-bed feature. Everywhere else in the community the Icarian motto, "All for each, each for all," was the invariable rule. If in the one matter of these tiny plots environing their humble domiciles, the Icarians allowed the idea of "meum et tuum" insidiously to enter, and if they found a keener enjoyment in the flowers or the grapes because of the forbidden but delicious sense of personal ownership, we must not condemn them too harshly, nor impeach their communism. There was something noble and pathetic in the manner with which these "citoyens" and "citoyennes" put away the accursed thing when they awoke to a realization of the fact that the gardens were introducing a dangerous element of individualism and inequality. This consciousness was arrived at about the time when the first half dozen of the new and more commodious houses were built ; and it was arranged that whenever a family should leave the hut for a frame-house, the wicked garden should be given up and no new ones should be made.[1] "Years rolled on," as the novelists say, and we come again to our point of departure, the inauspicious days of 1877. Three citizens still abode in

---

[1] It is somewhat interesting to note that this Icarian village community, in its tendency to evolve individual proprietorship, began precisely at the same point as the primitive village communities, which maintained common ownership and use of arable lands and pastures and woodlands long after the homesteads and their immediate environment had become individual property. Evidently the "petits jardins" are a modern reproduction of the ancient " toft and croft."

their primitive log-huts, and maintained, therefore, their "petits jardins." To the young party this was a scandal and an abomination ; nor did the old party really approve of the conduct of the three selfish citizens in clinging to their truck-patches and vines. In the fall of 1877 there was to be a sale of grapes; and a member of the young party proposed that, instead of gathering the fruit in the community's vineyard, there should be a confiscation of the grapes in the three little gardens. The proposition was certainly in keeping with Icarian principles. But the person who made it, and his manner of making it, were so offensive to the old party that they voted solidly against it.

All compromises were now at an end, and the factions were openly at war again. Sauva had by this time identified himself with the conservative party, and Peron had become the fluent spokesman of the "progressives," as they termed themselves. On the 26th of September the young party announced their fixed purpose to withdraw and found an autonomous branch on a portion of the domain, and a few days later they submitted a detailed plan by which the division might be accomplished. The land was to remain the common property of the two branches, but was to be assigned for use and control to the respective communes in a manner which they set forth in the following paragraph of their proposition :

" That a division of land and stock be made *pro rata*, each stockholder, man, woman, and child, to be given ten acres of land ; that henceforth we carry on our affairs, agricultural, industrial, and financial, as two distinct branches of one community ; that the land be held on both sides in usufruct only, each branch having the privilege of mortgaging its land to one fifth of its appraised valuation ; that each branch admit to its ranks such new members as it may deem proper (births being reckoned as new admissions); and that the surplus of land remaining after the division shall be made according to the above proposition, shall be held in common at the disposal of both sides for the use of its new members.   In case of death on either side, if the portion held in the name of the deceased is not taken up by a new admission within a specified time, the opposite party shall have the right to claim it."

The nineteen voters of the old party were emphatically opposed to the proposition, while, of course, the thirteen voters of the young party were agreed in urging it.   The plan certainly was a very awkward one, and must have led, if adopted, to continual friction and misunderstanding between the two communes.   Having thus failed to accomplish a separation in lawful manner by vote of the assembly, the " progressives " assumed a revolutionary attitude.   They might very easily have re-

signed and withdrawn, as at one time and another
in the history of Icaria many hundreds had done;
but they could have taken with them only a small
portion of the property. At this juncture the
Icarian constitution showed a singular weakness,
which was taken advantage of by the revolutionary
party. This faction had now resorted to the civil
courts, and was doing every thing in its power to
harass and destroy the community; and yet the
majority had no adequate defence, for the reason
that expulsion required a two-thirds vote, whereas
the rebellious minority cast one vote more than
three-eighths of the whole number. Though plot-
ting its destruction, the community was powerless
to expel them. The legal proceedings, which were
pending for some months, resulted in the forfeiture
by the Circuit Court of the Icarian charter, and the
appointment by Court of trustees to "wind up" the
business of the community.

Meanwhile many fruitless efforts at amicable
adjustment had been made. A new colony in some
remote region where personal frictions would be
avoided was a plan promptly rejected by the revo-
lutionists. Both parties devised plans of arbitration,
but in neither case could the preliminaries be agreed
upon.[1] The old party grew so generous as to offer

---

[1] The old people proposed that arbitrators should be selected from
among former Icarians, many of whom were scattered throughout the
West. They maintained that a dispute between Icarian factions
could best be understood and adjusted by those who had knowledge

their disaffected young compatriots a cash bonus
of several thousand dollars if they would withdraw
in peace and set up a community somewhere else.
But the young people had other plans.

It is, perhaps, not to be expected that, in a country where the property rights of the individual are
held more sacred by the laws than aught else,
scarcely excepting life and personal liberty, the
Courts should take into consideration the peculiar
nature of a property accumulated, and held through
an entire generation, on the principles of communism. Many an old member whose toil had helped
to build up the establishment, and whose donation
of his private possessions on joining the community
had added to the wealth of the society, had long
since died ; or perchance he had for personal reasons
withdrawn from membership, taking next to nothing
with him, but consoled by the thought that what he
had left behind would perpetually promote the
good cause of communism. The purpose and prin-

---

of and sympathy with Icarian principles. They thought the vital
issue should be settled on the basis of communistic and Icarian doctrines. On the other hand the young people proposed an arbitration
by "old settlers" of the county, *i. e.*, by their American farmer
neighbors. Now the only point of view possible for such arbitrators
must have been that of individual rights. With them separation
would have been a foregone conclusion. Their only care would have
been to secure an equitable distribution of the property among the
members. Certainly the young party were right in regarding this
plan as the most favorable to the end they had in view, that of separation ; while the plan proposed by the old folks was of course much
more in accord with the peculiar principles professed by both parties,
and much more likely to favor the object of the old party, that of
preserving intact the domain of the community.

ciple of Icaria was radically different from that of
an ordinary business corporation or joint-stock company. Except as recognized in a very limited way
in cases of withdrawal, there were really no individual rights in the property of the community.
Occupiers held only in trust, as it were, in a line of
perpetual succession. Unfortunately, under the
laws of Iowa they had been obliged to organize in
the form of a joint-stock company under the designation of an " agricultural society," and each member was nominally the holder of a share of stock.
The Court saw fit to hold the community strictly
and technically as a chartered business corporation.
The plan pursued by the minority was to secure the
abrogation of the charter by proving that the community had performed functions in excess or in violation of those granted. Of course the plaintiffs felt
themselves justified in using every influence and
every technicality to gain their end. Nevertheless,
it did seem a little surprising when they gravely
charged their elder brethren with being *communists*
forsooth, and with making the establishment of
communism the chief motive and purpose of their
organization, rather than the tilling of the soil and
the raising of live stock, as specified in their articles
of incorporation! When it is remembered that the
young party possessed several members fresh from
the Paris barricades of 1871, and that the complaint
against the old party all along had been its luke-

warm zeal for communism, and when one further
considers the wholesome horror that an Iowa jury
would be likely to experience when the word "communist" was mentioned in court,—these things
taken into account, one is in condition to appreciate
the fine humor of such an accusation. The forfeiture
of the charter seems finally to have been pronounced
by the Court on the ground that a society which was
incorporated for agricultural purposes had exceeded
its powers in constructing and operating a mill on
its estate, and in doing certain other things of a
mechanical and manufacturing character. The man-
ufacture of lumber and flour had really been a very
subordinate part of the industry of the community,
and the spirit of the charter had suffered no violation; for Icaria, even against the will of the
accusing party, had remained an agricultural community instead of becoming a manufacturing community. But the Court doubtless believed a recon-
ciliation to be hopeless, and being convinced that
substantial justice to all parties required the dissolution of the society, the technical ground already
named was made to justify a forfeiture of the charter. In 1856 the Cabet party at Nauvoo had tried
in vain to compass the abrogation of the Illinois
charter; and after Cabet's death, his heirs, probably
in behalf of the Cheltenham community, had fruit-
lessly attempted to secure the real estate, the titles
to which were in Cabet's name. Certainly the com-

munity had better cause to expect protection from the law in 1878 than in those former suits. The decision disregarded the nature of the Icarian estate as a perpetual foundation, with its own definite provision for the withdrawal of discontented members,—a foundation in which were involved the rights of hundreds of predecessors and the rights of an indeterminate number of prospective successors, as well as the rights of those immediately on the ground and which alone were regarded. Possibly the current feeling against communism, vague but strong, made the Court the more willing to reduce Icaria to its constituent atoms.

On the 17th of August, 1878, the Circuit Court declared the charter forfeited, and appointed three trustees, who were charged with the task of an equitable distribution of the property. By mutual agreement between the factions, these trustees were superseded by a board of arbitrators chosen among the American neighbors ; and during the months of January and February, 1879, this board held sessions attended by the delegates from the two parties. In their apportionment the arbitrators took account of the amount individuals had originally deposited with the community, and the period of their service as members. Somewhat more than half of the property fell to the party of the old people. Meanwhile, it was understood that each wing would reorganize as a separate community, and it was arranged that the domain should be divided into eastern and western portions, the old party remaining in the original village, and the young people building a new hamlet a mile to the eastward, where they had asked leave to colonize themselves two years before.

# VII.

## REÖRGANIZATION—"THE NEW ICARIAN COMMUNITY."

# VII.

IT was expected that the old party would retain the old name and keep the old domicile; but it happened otherwise. The young people were somewhat more prompt in their reörganization, and on the 16th of April they were the possessors of a new charter under the ancient title of "The Icarian Community." The conservative ex-majority took the name of "The New Icarian Community"; and upon receipt of a bonus of fifteen hundred dollars from their successful adversaries, they consented to become the emigrants, and accepted the eastern portion of the domain for their new home. There, with a patience and courage which enemies could but respect, they took up the broken threads of community life, and quietly restored the order of their social economy.

For President they chose Marchand, who had suffered with the first advance guard in Texas in 1848, and had ever since been a leading Icarian. They built a new dining and assembly hall similar to the one in the old village, and grouped about it eight of the frame cottages which had been assigned to them in

the division of goods, and which they removed
bodily from the other hamlet.

The subjoined diagram will show the plan of
New Icaria :

(Trees and Park.)

(Hall.)

The group of houses stands upon a level plateau
many acres in extent, and commanding a view un-
usually varied and charming for a prairie State.
From the plateau the land slopes gradually to the
meadows flanking the Nodaway, a mile to the north-
ward. The stream is fringed with trees, and its
winding course across the prairie is revealed for
many miles by the waving timber line, now a mere
fringe of underbrush, and now widening into a considerable grove. On the bank directly north of the
hamlet is to be seen the mill, which in the partition
fell to the portion of the old party. Half-way
between the village and the mill passes the railroad.
East and south of the village recede long stretches
of rolling prairie, broken now into farms. To the
west, among the trees, lies the old village ; and
still further west, on the horizon, are the more
ambitious uplands beyond the Nodaway, on the
slopes of which a glimpse may be had of the town
of Corning. Here, in the summer of 1879, some

thirty Icarians resumed the seemingly discouraging experiment of communistic life.

In the spring and again in the fall of 1883 it was my privilege to spend several days among them there. Their numbers had remained almost stationary, and amounted now to thirty-four, including twelve men, ten women, and twelve children all under thirteen years of age. In spite of its hardships, Icarian life has proved remarkably conducive to health and longevity; and eight of the thirty-four people were past the age of sixty. While in one sense the whole community constituted one family, there was not wanting something of a private home-life in each of the humble cottages, in which one was sure to find books and papers, with perhaps a bird-cage hanging in the window, or a quaint picture or two on the plain walls. With no carpets, the scantiest furniture, and a sad lack of the small household accessories, these neat and tidy Frenchwomen had managed to give an air of decency and even of comfort to their little homes. Quite regardless of the old scruple against the "petits jardins," a number of bright flower-beds environed the houses. The park upon which the cottages fronted had been laid out with some care and taste, and promised to be a charming place when the trees were grown. Young vineyards and orchards were flourishing. A large kitchen-garden supplied abundance of all ordinary greens and vegetables, together with a great variety

of extraordinary kinds known only to Frenchmen.
The fare in the common dining-hall was wholesome,
though not served in an elaborate manner. The
visitor could not fail to be impressed by the intelligence of every one, the pleasant and polite manners
of the women, and the bright and pretty appearance
of the children.

In dress the Icarians are necessarily very plain,
though entirely free from the affectation of peculi-
arities. At Nauvoo, when the colony numbered
some hundreds, there was more reason for adopting
uniformity of garb than in the small community of
to-day where there is no temptation to extrava-
gance or to rivalry in dress. A dark blue calico is
the fabric most commonly worn by the women on
week-days. The men wear the plain, substantial
clothes of western farmers. Most of the members
can converse in English, but French is used exclusively in the community, and it is spoken with great
accuracy and purity. The government is, of course,
purely democratic. The functionaries are a President, a Secretary and Treasurer, and three Directors, all of whom are chosen annually, on the third
of February, the anniversary of the first departure
from Havre. The President represents the society
in its external affairs, and the Directors have charge
respectively of agriculture, industry, clothing and
lodging. The Director of Industry is superintend-
ent of buildings, fences, the mill, etc. A woman is

generally chosen Director of Clothing and Lodging. The acts of all these officers are subject to discussion and revision in the general assembly, which holds frequent sessions; and in more important matters, the officers simply carry into effect the decisions of the assembly. The women are entitled to vote on several questions, such as the admission of new members, amendments to the constitution, choice of a Director of Clothing and Lodging, and some other matters either of more than ordinary importance or of more than usual concern to the women themselves. On most current questions they do not vote.

The community has its own tailor and shoemaker, but otherwise little is attempted besides agriculture. The land of the New Icarian Community amounts to about eleven hundred acres, of which two hundred are woodland. Since an abundance of good coal has been found in the county, timber land has not the relative value it once had, especially as very few of the trees are suitable for sawing into lumber. Fuel and fencing material comprise the total product of the timber land. The sawmill has ceased therefore to yield much income, and stands idle most of the time. The same is also true of the flouring mill which is under the same roof. The agriculture is of the usual western character, corn and hay being the principal crops, and cattle and hogs the chief marketable products.

The amusements of the community are not of a very gay and hilarious character, and are not so prominent a feature of the social life as they would be, were the young members more numerous. (Although we have generally referred to this branch as the " *old* party," it was not exclusively composed of old people ; on the other hand the party of the young people contained several aged persons.) The younger members have some musical taste, and there is a cabinet organ in the hall. The library, now containing about a thousand volumes—an equal number having been kept at the other village, —consists chiefly of standard French works of literature, philosophy, history, science, and miscellany, most of them saved from the wreck of the Nauvoo library. A number of French and American periodicals are taken, and their perusal is the favorite recreation. Sunday is kept as a holiday, and sometimes the little community gathers in the assembly hall for music, select reading, a dance, or an amateur play; while on other Sundays a quiet picnic is enjoyed under the trees on the Nodaway. The standard of morality is high, and the ethical sense of the community, trained by their unselfish mode of life, is superior; but, though permitting any form of belief among their members, they are not religious. Being materialists and positivists, philosophically, they exalt their communistic doctrines into a so-called religion of humanity. Cabet's views of the life and character of Jesus Christ, as presented in his "Vrai Christianisme," are those held by the Icarians to-day.

Their relations with the outside world show admirable discretion and good sense. If a marriage is to take place, the nearest justice of the peace is resorted to, and the knot is tied in a simple and legal manner. The school-house, which stands midway between the two villages and is patronized by both, belongs in the regular district school system of the county, and school-director and teacher are chosen in the usual manner. As there are only two or three families besides Icarians resident in the school-district, an Icarian is always elected director, and the teacher is appointed with particular reference to the character of the school. For several years an intelligent French lady, well educated in Cincinnati, and formerly an Icarian, has presided in the school-room. Until quite recently Icaria maintained its own schools, wherein Icarian doctrines, manners, and morals received much attention; but the depleted membership of the communities has of late years made the present arrangement expedient.

From the first the Icarians have been good American citizens, taking a quiet but intelligent part in public affairs, and showing high respect for our institutions and forms of government. Cabet and all his comrades took out naturalization papers in 1848, and showed ardent sympathy with abolitionist and free-soil doctrines. They voted the Fremont presidential ticket in 1856, and Marchand is rather proud of having voted for every Republican President. All his fellow-members in the New Icarian Community remain Republicans. The other community has for several years thrown its political influence with the "Greenback" party on the ground that it represents dissatisfaction with the present state of society. If the colony had remained in Texas, its thorough-going ideas of liberty must have involved it in trouble with its neighbors,[1] and the war would have endangered its existence. A number of its members saw military service in the Union Army. They wisely keep aloof from the strife of politics, and enter its domain only as simple voters. An Icarian occasionally fills a township administrative office, but never is a candidate for any position the duties of which would interfere with his community life and work.

As money-getters, the people of New Icaria are only moderately successful. However, by frugal living and faithful labor, they are reducing and will

---

[1] Mr. Marchand informs me that the pioneer party in Texas in 1848, were everywhere asked if they were Democrats. Their ignorance of the English language was only surpassed by their profound ignorance of American party distinctions. Of course they replied unhesitatingly that they were "democrats," as they certainly had been in France ; and for some reason not then understood by them they found that this profession of political faith made the Louisianians and Texans uncommonly kind. Mr. Marchand thinks the Democratic party wins the adherence of a great many foreigners simply on account of the prepossession they bring in favor of the word "democrat."

soon extinguish the debt in which their expensive quarrel and their re-establishment involved them. On the 1st of January, 1883, the property of New Icaria was worth at a very low estimate $25,000; and their indebtedness approached $4,000. Their land is steadily appreciating in value, and one or two good crops will pay the debt and leave them in a financial condition which will amply justify the admission of new members and will permit the introduction of many comforts and luxuries now painfully lacking. Of their business policy and manner of labor, one who knew the Icarians before the separation, made the following remarks, which are quite applicable to New Icaria to-day: "Having learned from bitter experience that debt is the bane of societies, as well as of individuals, the Icarians have adopted it as a fixed principle, to contract no liabilities, and to avoid all speculative and hazardous enterprises. They are content with small gains, and in an old-fashioned way study rather to moderate their outlays than to increase their profits. Naturally, as they own in common, they are not in haste to be rich. With them the acquisition of wealth is not a leading object of life. They have greater regard to independence, and give more thought to personal ease. They labor industriously, but not exhaustingly, and in such ways as to make their toil as comfortable and pleasant as possible."[1]

---

[1] S. W. Moorhead in *The Western Magazine*, Omaha, July, 1877.

To keep the world apprised of its doings the community issues a small monthly paper the *Revue Icarienne*, which is printed on a curious and antiquated little press—originally a lithograph press—brought from France by the early colonists. An edition of about three hundred copies is printed. These circulate among French people of Icarian antecedents in the United States, and in France among the friends of the colonists.

Such, in brief, is an outline of the *modus vivendi* prevailing in New Icaria, as it has come under my observation. It is a plain, monotonous life; yet I cannot hesitate to affirm that it seems in some respects a more rational and intelligent life than that which is to be found in the average American farmhouse of the West. Certainly a more serene life one will not often discover any where, in this age of turmoil, haste, and discontent.

In their reorganization both parties undertook to provide against the recurrence of deadlocks and constitutional crises, but resorted to different expedients. The New Icarian Community (the old people), instead of filing articles of incorporation under the State law, decided to organize in the form of a general partnership. They drew up a comprehensive Contract of Partnership which they all duly signed and which was placed on record in the office of the County Recorder. This organization was found to give the community all the practical advantages of an incorporated body, while avoiding some of the dangers and disadvantages. The contract is itself so satisfactory a statement of Icarian principles and of their ordinary modes of government, as well also as of their constitutional provisions for the protection of the society in case of future dissensions, that I have made a translation of it and added it as an appendix.[1]

So far as the form of organization can protect a society and provide safeguards against its dissolution, New Icaria seems to be well fortified by the main provisions of this contract. Each member agrees to relinquish all individual claims and to refrain from any attempt at any time to recover a portion of the property. Permission is given to a majority to expel a minority when in an overt state of rebellion or insubordination. Under articles of incorporation the society might at any time be dissolved for some technical violation of its charter on the information of an outsider ; but under this contract of partnership no outside interference is possible. But safeguards like these, while they may assure the *existence* of New Icaria for a long time to come, cannot give it life and success. The evils of stagnation are now more to be feared in New Icaria than those of dissension. If the jealousy of personal leadership could be laid aside, and if some strong man gifted with executive ability and full of

---

[1] See Appendix I.

enthusiasm could be entrusted with the direction of affairs, an auspicious future might yet await the society.   As it is, predictions would be worthless and superfluous.

# VIII.

## "LA JEUNE ICARIE."

# VIII.

THE new Articles of Incorporation under which the young party reorganized on the 16th of April, 1879, took care to provide against the fate of the old charter by stating the nature and purpose of the organization in terms so inclusive as to render it practically impossible for the community to exceed its lawful powers. Article II. reads as follows: "This corporation, having for its object the mutual support of each other, and the creating of a fund with which to provide for the comfort of the young, the old, the sick, and decrepit, and the carrying out of the principles set forth in the preamble hereof [welfare and happiness of humanity and demonstration of the feasibility of community life]; for that purpose the general nature of business to be transacted shall be all kinds of agriculture, horticulture, stock-raising, mechanical arts of every kind and nature, milling, manufacturing in all its departments, and the establishment and building of towns, villages, colonies, schools, and colleges, also the development of the fine arts and also all kinds of commerce." The articles provide that upon withdrawal members shall receive the amount of property actually paid in by them, less a proportion of the indebtedness of the society, and shall further receive such sums for years of service as the by-laws of the corporation may specify. To show, however, that this liberal provision for a return to the selfish life of the world was not for their own benefit but rather for the reassurance and comfort of new-comers, the incorporators at once proceeded to draw up what they entitled an "Act of Donation to the Icarian Community," by which they relin-quished all personal claim upon the property. The essential paragraphs in this act of donation are as follows :

"Know all men by these presents that we : Antoi-nette Cubels, Thérèse James, Louise Bettannier, Marie Mourot, Madeleine Vallet, Valentine Vallet, Louise Peron, Léonie Dereure, Francoise Leroux, Adèle Gau-vain, Emilie Fugier, Maria Laforgue, Henriette Vallet, Caroline Gauvain, Jean Hægen, Michael Brumme, An-toine Gauvain, Emile Fugier, Alexis Marchand, Simon Dereure, Jérôme Laforgue, Paul Leroux, Emile Peron, Eugène Mourot, Pierre James, Justin Vallet, Auguste Gauvain, Alexandre Vallet, being members of the Icarian Community of Adams County, Iowa, and being desirous of promoting its interests, and of establishing a perpetual fund for the promotion of the business and principles of said Corporation, do hereby donate, assign, and set over, unto the said Corporation, each for ourselves, the several sums, property, rights, and credits as follows, to wit :

"All our right, title, and interest unto the several sums, subscribed by us, on the books of said Corporation, being the property and interest received by us as our share of the old Corporation of Icarian Community, and which we were found to be entitled to by a board of arbitration that was selected to settle up between the members of the old Icarian Community ; the same to be held by said Corporation to them and their successors forever, never to be divided between the individual members of said Corporation under any circumstances whatever ; but to be used by the Corporation for the general purposes of its organization, and in case said Corporation shall for any reason dissolve, and fails to keep its organization renewed from time to time, upon such dissolution the above amount as donated, after the payment of debts of the Corporation, shall be accounted for and paid over to any number of Icarians, who shall become incorporated on the same principles and for the same purposes as are set forth in the Articles and By-Laws of this Corporation."

In the following October Icaria adopted a new constitution which, in the picturesque phraseology of a member, " extends the right of suffrage to women, abolishes the presidency, overthrows the demi-gods and their Jacobin notions of political infallibility, associates the efforts of the community with those of outside socialistic agitation, formulates the Icarian creed according to rationalism founded on observation, and places it outside of and against all anti-scientific revelations." This consti-

tution, which abounds in felicitous and epigrammatic
expressions pointing to Mr. Peron as its author, is
a rather remarkable document. It has a long
preface discussing the history of society and maintaining the philosophical and scientific basis of
socialism. The second chapter sets forth in twenty-
six articles the general principles of the community
on the subjects of Society, Equality, Liberty, Fraternity, Unity, and Law. The third chapter is concerned with Social Organization, and states the views
of the society as to community of property; the
education of the young; the institution of marriage,
which is approved; voluntary celibacy, which is dis-
approved. The fourth chapter deals with the
Political Organization. The government is as purely
democratic as possible, and the office of President
is given up. The only officers are four Trustees,
two of whom are elected semi-annually. One of
these is Secretary-Treasurer, and the others have
charge respectively of Industry, Agriculture, and
Commerce. These Trustees execute the mandates
of the general assembly. Various matters of detail
are entrusted from time to time by the general assembly to special commissions appointed and em-
powered as the occasion requires. The general
assembly is itself the government. It is not to be
presided over by one of the Trustees, but by a chair-
man selected anew at each meeting. The constitution states that " it is the duty of the Community

to set apart such sums of money as it may deem necessary to the propagation of principles which tend to the political, philosophical, and economic emancipation of mankind," and to this end a standing committee of propagandism is provided for.

For the information of the public and the convenience of applicants and inquirers, a pamphlet was published containing this constitution and other laws and regulations of the Icarian Community. The " Law upon Admission " and the " Law upon Withdrawal and Expulsion " are particularly full and minute, and they contain so much of frank confession and sage reflection, under the head of " preliminary considerations," upon the difficulties of a community life, the differences between Utopian visions and existing realities, and the inevitable embarrassments of a sudden transition from the individualistic to the socialistic life, that it is thought worth while to publish them as an appendix.[1]

Young Icaria, freed from the apron-strings of the conservative party, set in order its household economy with some flourish and a great deal of real energy. During the period of discord and interregnum between the decision of the court and the reorganization, a number of people withdrew altogether. Of the eighty persons in the society before its dissolution, forty-seven belonged to the young party and thirty-three to the old, although as has been ex-

---

[1] See Appendix II.

plained, the latter party had a voting majority.
Having paid their elders an indemnity to withdraw,
the young party, with a total personnel of about
thirty-five, largely women and children, found themselves in undisputed control of the old village. Their
enthusiasm proved contagious, and applications for
admission came by the score. Before the end of
1880 there were upward of seventy names on the
roll of membership, including those admitted provisionally. Good crops blessed their labor. The
orchards and vineyards planted by the fathers were
now yielding bountifully for the sons. Advanced
methods in agriculture and stock-raising were
eagerly adopted. The industrial branch of production was begun with a shoe-shop and a blacksmith-
shop in the neighboring town of Corning, and a
broom factory was started. All labored with a fine
energy for a reduction of the debt of seven or eight
thousand dollars with which the community
property was encumbered.

Peron made *La Jeune Icarie*, the organ of the
community, a bright and able paper. He found
some time for scientific experiments. In the winter
he taught the inter-communal school; and the
electric telephone by which he connected the school-
house and his own cottage was the first one used in
the State. Among the new members were men of
intellect and experience. The communistic world
has its own channels of communication; and the

new vigor and promise of Icaria became known in the communistic world. Ten applicants knocked at the gate where one could be admitted. The community had only eight hundred acres of land, and so long as its industry was chiefly agricultural, membership could only be increased gradually, and could not safely pass a certain limit. Consequently it was the design of the society to develop a variety of industrial enterprises as speedily as circumstances would allow. The "Act of Donation," as an evidence of sincere devotion to the cause, had been highly approved by the communistic world, and young Icaria was enjoying an enviable reputation. And certainly its society was not to be despised. It had men who had seen military service on two continents; men who knew languages, history, philosophy, and modern science; men who could discuss current thought and were familiar with current literature; men who had seen experience in other communistic societies; old Icarians who had come back after years of absence; agreeable women, and plenty of vigorous infants.

So constituted, Icaria seemed to give promise of speedy and interesting achievements; but the promise, unfortunately, was not to be realized,—at least not without some adversity and delay. Under the first flush of excitement and novelty, the community had seemed to be of one heart and one mind; but when the group had become fairly accustomed to their surroundings and to one another, little inharmonies and incompatibilities began to appear. Decided differences of opinion as to the general policy of the community were found to be entertained. There were too many clever men, and no one with a gift of leadership sufficient to assimilate and unify the group. To use a favorite Icarian word, there was no real "solidarity." There were no bitter party quarrels, there was no "crisis," nor even much unfriendliness ; but the most of the new-comers soon deemed it expedient to withdraw, and the community was, in a year or two, reduced to a membership of about thirty, most of whom were of the original "young party" who had formed the incorporation and made the "Act of Donation." Of those who departed, some went into private life ; a family or two went to Florida with the purpose of founding there a colony on Icarian principles ; and in the spring of 1881 a group of families went to California to inaugurate a community enterprise which will again have mention in these annals.

So many members having departed, it became for the present unprofitable to give attention to its new industrial enterprises, and the shops in Corning were given up, the community merely providing for its own needs in small shops on its own estate. The cultivation of corn and the cereals on a large scale was also given up, and the land was seeded to grass for the maintenance of flocks and herds, stock-farming having been found more profitable and less toilsome than plowing and sowing and reaping. But our friends were already becoming convinced that the business of general farming and stock-feeding in a Northern State is not the one best adapted to the welfare of a community like theirs. A certain amount of leisure for mental improvement must be regarded as an indispensable condition of success in a society based on Icarian or similar principles. Community life must provide something besides bread and butter, or it falls short of its main object. The young Icarians came to have a painful feeling that for them the arduous business of general farming was an impediment in the way of moral and intellectual progress, and they began to look forward to a removal at some time to a warmer climate, where horticulture, a business so congenial to the Frenchman, might take the place of heavy farming, which seldom suits the Gallic temperament.

Florida was talked of, and those who had gone thither sent glowing accounts of orange and lemon groves and cheap lands. A committee which was sent out to "prospect" for a location visited Kentucky, Tennessee, Louisiana, and the neighborhood of the original Icarian station in Texas, now a flourishing region. The group of families who went to California had purchased a tract of fruit-land in

Sonoma County, eighteen miles from San Francisco, and were sending enthusiastic reports from the occident, and were inviting their former associates in Iowa to join them. At length it came to be generally understood that the community would leave Iowa whenever a favorable opportunity to sell the property should be found, and would resort to the pleasant fruit-lands of California. Under these circumstances plans of enlargement and improvement were for the time postponed, and attempts at propaganda were held in abeyance. The future triumphs or failures of the community were not to be in Iowa.

# IX.

## IN CALIFORNIA—"ICARIA-SPERANZA."

# IX.

AT length, in the winter of 1883–4, the negotiations which had been for some time pending, resulted in the adoption of a definite basis and contract of union between the little Icarian group at Cloverdale, California, and the Icarian community (young branch) in Iowa. It was agreed that as soon as Icaria could dispose of the Iowa estate, its members would remove in a body to California and unite fortunes with their friends on the " Bluxome rancho."

Of the interesting personal history of the little group already in California something more will be said in a subsequent chapter devoted to the portraiture of various Icarians. Suffice it to say here that the leader of the colony was a Mr. Dehay, the son-in-law of an aged exile of '48, Jules Leroux, and that the sons of the latter, Pierre Leroux and Jules Leroux *fils*, with their families, with two or three additional families not of the Leroux connection, made up the entire membership. These families had left Icaria in the spring of 1881, and had wisely spent several months in California before deciding upon a purchase. In September they found for sale the

Bluxome ranch on the Russian river, in Sonoma County, two or three miles from the town of Cloverdale, and eighteen miles from San Francisco. It contained 885 acres, and suited them precisely. The price demanded was $15,000. Mr. Dehay was possessed of upward of $4,000, and the others were able to contribute enough to make up the first payment of $5,000. The remaining payments were considerably deferred, and the little colony set vigorously to work to pay the debt. At the end of two years they had a farm worth $30,000 and their debt was reduced to $6,000. Though living in an associative way, they had not yet framed a formal and legal organization, that being deferred in anticipation of some such event as the fusion with the young Icarian commune.

For a description of the character and capabilities of the farm, and its charms of situation, I may quote from an article which an editor in the neighboring town of Cloverdale inserted in his paper in December, 1882.[1]

" Two miles and one half below town, skirting the banks of our beautiful stream, Russian River, lies the extensive farm owned by the French colonists. * * * The commodious dwellings and barns are located on the Healdsburg road, where they were erected several years ago, and present a rare picture of rural comfort. Sweeping around over low, rolling hills and smiling valleys, is seen the body of the farm, which is destined in the near

---

[1] *The Pacific Sentinel,* Cloverdale, Dec. 21, 1882.

future to become one of the finest vineyards in California. The entire tract comprises 885 acres, of which about 400 is first-class vineyard land that is being rapidly cleared and made ready for the plow. Nine white men and six Chinamen are at work grubbing out trees and brush, preparing the land for cultivation, and acre after acre is rapidly being added to the improved area. At present, forty-five acres are planted in rooted vines, principally of the Zin-fandel variety, and enough will be added in the spring to swell the area to fifty acres. * * * Besides the vineyard, one hundred acres of fair-grade wheat land is under cultivation, and at this writing it is all sown and some of the young grain is already above ground. A thrifty orchard of five acres stretches to the west from the Healdsburg road, and includes many choice varieties of trees. Some of the finest peaches we have ever tasted were produced here. * * * It is the intention of the proprietors to increase the area of the orchard as soon as possible, and they will engage extensively in the culture of French and German prunes. They intend planting nothing but the very best varieties, and hence will make a success of the business. They also propose establishing a first-class winery and distillery as soon as their production will admit of the outlay. As soon as practicable a French colony will be formed, duly incorporated, to include some twenty-five families, and with this force the large farm will soon be developed. * * * The site on which the dwellings intended for the colonists will be built, is located near the road in a beautiful meadow, sloping on a gentle incline to the banks of the Russian River, and is one of the most beautiful spots in this locality.

" Standing on a vine-planted mound near the road, and gazing upon the beautiful valley, which will one day be the centre for so much life and prosperity, we must admit that it is naturally an earthly Eden.  Geyser Peak stands boldly forth at no great distance from the lovely vale, and even Mt. St. Helena is plainly visible, towering toward heaven in the distance.  The low hills on every side, the road winding along and almost parallel here with the curving river, the picturesque woods and the smiling vineyards, all unite in forming a panorama transcendant in its quiet, peaceful beauty.  Exclusive of vineyard and grain land, there yet remains about three hundred acres of rolling hill-land, suitable for pasture, and the colonists will utilize this by entering the cattle-raising business. They thoroughly understand this class of ranching, and prefer it to wool-growing."

As thus described, the topography and the capabilities of the new Icarian station are most inviting. Certainly, if the writer were seeking the realization of a Utopia, his ideal would not be met in a community of factory operatives, nor of toiling agriculturists engaged in the rough labor of general farming in a Northern State; but of all places and all occupations on earth he would choose as most consonant with the theories and purposes of communism—California and horticulture.  In beginning life anew on the Pacific slope, an Icarian commune for the first time finds itself in an environment thoroughly favorable to its development. Few persons outside of California have yet come to realize the marvels of its orchard products and the "terrestrial Paradises" in which its opulent horticulturists embower themselves. An acre there produces more fruit, and of vastly superior quality, than ten or twenty acres elsewhere in the United States. The soberest recital of facts concerning the transformation, during the past decade, of wide tracts of California wheat-lands into orchards and gardens containing all the fruits and spices of the tropics in addition to all the fruits of the temperate regions, seems too extravagant for belief. Yet it is true that lands which a few years ago, as wheat-fields, gave employment to four men, now require at least four hundred fruit-gatherers during the picking season; and the tract which, in wheat, furnished a comfortable income to a single proprietor, now enables fifty proprietors to live in comfort and refinement as fruit-growers.

Taking, therefore, the roseate view of the future of the "Icaria-Speranza Community," as the fusion of the two groups is to be called, it is not hard to imagine that in a few years they will have transformed the Bluxome ranch into a veritable Paradise; that in place of the primitive sheds of the Texas pioneers, the tenements of the sojourners at Nauvoo, the log-huts or the box-like frame structures in Iowa, the Icarians will dwell in commodious and beautiful houses with complete appointments somewhat after the manner of those pictured by Cabet

in the "Voyage en Icarie"; that the educational
and recreational, the scientific and literary, pursuits
so highly esteemed by the Icarians will have found
their long-deferred opportunity to flourish; that the
climate and the nature of the work will have proved
remarkably adapted to the French temperament,
and that membership will have increased rapidly,
both from within and from without. Indeed, the
very necessity of many active hands to gather in
the fruit will compel the increase of membership as
the area of orchard and vineyard increases; and in
work of this kind the women and children are as
useful as men. On the other hand, the enforced
leisure of six or eight months in the year will prove
advantageous to the mental and moral interests of
the community. But even while picturing this
attractive prospect, one can hardly help remember-
ing the unpleasant occurrences which were disas-
trous to the first Paradise of which we read; and
judging their future by their past, what guaranty
can we have that our French friends will love one
another and behave themselves discreetly in their
Paradise? Alas, there is the rub!

The new name, "Icaria-Speranza," was adopted
as a compromise. The Messrs. Leroux were attached to the name "Speranza" because their uncle,
the famous philosopher, Pierre Leroux, had given
that title to a Utopian romance he had published,
in which he pictured a social organization somewhat

like that advocated by Cabet. The name " Icaria-Speranza " perpetuates, therefore, the memories and unites the similar social systems of two distinguished contemporaneous writers and radical politicians, Etiénne Cabet and Pierre Leroux.

The new constitution of " Icaria-Speranza " is in the form of a " Contract and Articles of Agreement." Like the " New Icarian Community," they have concluded that the form of a general partnership is preferable to that of a corporation. This new constitution contains many important innovations; and as it is the fruit of the combined reflection and experience of men who know well the problems of community life, it is worth careful study.[1] Among the cardinal principles of the old Icarian constitution were these three: 1, the absolute authority of the majority except in a few specified cases ; 2, the absolute community of property ; 3, the absolute control of the individual by the society—*i. e.*, the abnegation of personal liberty. The new constitution considerably modifies these three principles, as we shall proceed to show, after having explained the framework of the government. The General Assembly is composed of all full members of both sexes, above the age of twenty-one. In January of each year, five standing committees are elected, having charge of the following subjects : 1, Works ; 2, Home Consumption ; 3, Education ; 4,

---

[1] This constitution will be found in full as Appendix III.

Commerce ; 5, Accounts. These committees in a collective capacity constitute the Board of Administration. The Board has vested in it the titles to the property of the community. Ordinary matters of administration are attended to by the individual committees, or if more important, by the entire Board. Regular meetings of the General Assembly are held only twice a year ; though special meetings may be called at any time by the Board, or by a certain number of members concurring in a written request. *No action whatever can be taken by a committee, or by the Board of Administration, unless with the unanimous consent of every member of such Committee or Board ; and no decision of the General Assembly is valid unless sustained by a three-fourths vote.* In many matters,such as admissions, expulsions, etc., a nine-tenths vote of the whole voting membership is required. To amend or change certain of the Articles of Agreement, a unanimous vote is requisite, for other articles a nine-tenths vote, and for the rest a three-fourths vote. The evident object is to have as little government as possible, and to leave routine administration to the committees instead of discussing every detail in frequent meetings of the assembly. This will have a marked tendency to mitigate that bane of communities,—too much politics. While majority tyranny will evidently be impossible, minority conservatism may at times block the wheels of progress. But this power of the minority can be exercised only negatively—*i. e.*, as a veto power; and the intention that changes shall not be made without a very general concurrence of view, would seem favorable to the stability of the society. Party action under this system will have much less scope than under the old majority rule. A useful device to facilitate elections of officers is introduced. For election on the first ballot a three-fourths majority of all the voting membership is requisite; on second ballot a simple majority elects ; and on third ballot the person receiving the highest number of votes—that is, a plurality—is elected.

But the greatest innovation in this new constitution lies in the admission, to a limited extent, of the principle of private property. Each family is to have exclusive and absolute ownership in articles of apparel, furniture, and in general in the equipments and utensils of the household. This will give greater freedom and independence to personal and family life. Up to an annual value of fifty dollars, individuals may receive, and keep as their own, presents from friends outside the organization. The book-keeping of the community is to provide in the following way for the contingency of withdrawal : Upon entering the community, individuals place all their property in the common fund, and the amount is credited upon the books. An inventory is taken at the end of every year, and the surplus, or net profits, is calculated. This sum is divided into two equal parts, one of which goes to augment the common indivisible fund, and the other is divided into as many equal shares as there are voting members, such shares being credited on the individual accounts in the community's books. This, however, is not so great a departure from communism as it might at first seem; for no one has any right or claim to the sums placed to his credit until he has relinquished all his membership rights, and has actually returned to the world and its ways; in which case this method of book-keeping readily determines the amount that shall be paid him. Of course under this constitution the famous "Icarian Donation" is still respected, and the most of the charter members would not be entitled to withdraw their original deposit in case they should retire, although they would be entitled to the annual sums placed to their credit, and also to a bonus of two hundred dollars provided for, to meet their case, in an article of the new contract.

The feature of this constitution most open to criticism is that of the so-called "labor-premiums." To each person above the age of sixteen who engages in the common work of the community, there is to be paid a monthly "labor-premium" of one dollar and a half, provided he has lost no working-time. If he has lost not more than half a day in the month, he will receive one dollar; and if not more than a day, fifty cents. No excuses whatsoever will be accepted in lieu of lost time. The Icarians are neither hermits nor fanatics ; and from the nature of their surroundings they must come so much in contact with the outside world, as to make a little private spending-money a convenient thing. Furthermore, in the theory of communism there can be no serious objection to having such spending-money, provided the distribution of it is not upon objectionable principles. This plan of labor-premiums would seem designed to reward good health and a mere show of "putting in the time." The man who is sick a day, or who is kept from work by reason of sickness in his family, may have served the community during the other days of the month in such a way as to be ten times as valuable as another who has lost no time ; yet the former sacrifices his pittance of spending-money. " From each according to his abilities, to each according to his needs," is the original Icarian motto ; and this labor-premium arrangement is not at all consistent with it. One might infer that the chief practical difficulty in a communistic society arose from the disposition of members to shirk steady labor ; and yet as a matter of fact that is not the case. With the possible exception of Robert Owen's motley congregation at New Harmony, no community has ever been troubled in that way. With all their other adverse experiences, the Icarians have never been annoyed by the presence of lazy members. An atmosphere

of industry pervades community life which is practically irresistible in its influence.   There seems no
good reason whatever why the distribution of a
little pocket-money once a month should be made
upon so arbitrary and unreasonable a plan.   In our
opinion the labor-premiums will be found impracti-
cable, and will in time be superseded by a simple
and even-handed method of distributing from time
to time among all faithful members such sums as
may seem desirable.

The matter of clothing illustrates the greater personal freedom permitted by the new constitution.
Instead of furnishing necessary articles of raiment
without regard to individual choice, the Board of
Administration will open accounts in the name of
each individual member with merchants in the
neighboring town ; and each may buy such clothing
as pleases him, within the limits of the sum placed
to his credit for that purpose.   Parents provide for
their children on the same plan.   The credit is to
be renewed twice a year, the " budget" being prepared by the Committee of Home Consumption,
and subjected to the approval of the Assembly.   For
other interesting features of this constitution, the
reader is referred to the document itself.[1]

The following extract from a letter written me by
Mr. Peron is a good general comment upon the new
instrument :

---

[1] See appendix III.

"We have abandoned the legal form of a corporation, and have adopted that of a general partnership, living under the clauses of a covenant containing a good many more provisos for liberty than our former constitution does. * * * We consider the adoption of our new *modus vivendi* as a pacific revolution in Icaria. We have all lost the greater part of our faith in the principles of majority rule, and adhere more every day to the higher doctrine of assent by all to any act affecting common interest. Therefore we reject all the more the primitive notions of leadership, temporal or spiritual, have no use for Presidents, high-titled officials, etc., and rely mostly upon everybody's sense of duty and responsibility to keep our machine a-going morally and materially. In fine, it is our first leap in the brilliant avenue which leads to social anarchy—understood in its good sense—or to the very attractive doctrine of ' Do as you please,' so cleverly and humanely expounded by our immortal French philosopher, Rabelais. Of course narrow minds, the commonplace tribe of grocers, will call it a mad leap ; but we except, stating that we know our high business as well as they understand theirs, which is limited to the very small circumference of a hysteric dollaromania."

The material prospects of Icaria-Speranza are decidedly good. The community begins with an aggregate capital of about $60,000. Besides its fruit-culture and wine business, it will engage in the breeding of blooded live stock, and will have good expectations of a bountiful income after a season or two of preparation. The combined membership at

present is fifty-two.   Such is the Icarian movement
in its latest phase.   There is no middle ground for
" Icaria-Speranza " ; it must be either a bright success
or a dismal failure.   Which it shall be will depend,
not upon external conditions, but upon the devotion,
forbearance, harmony, and what in general we may
term the associative capacity of its members.

# X.

## PERSONAL SKETCHES.

# X.

A BOOK might be filled with sketches of the re-markable men who have at one time or another been connected with Icaria. Thus, of the colony in its palmy days at Nauvoo some one has written: "A physician who had received diplomas from two German universities, and an ex-military officer who had won distinction in Algiers and had been decorated with the cross of the Legion of Honor, were enrolled in the corps of wood-choppers. A civil engineer who had superintended the construction of a great French railroad was put in charge of the wheezy old engine of the flouring mill. An accomplished young architect and builder from Normandy was retained by the President as a private secretary, and spent most of his time rendering Cabet's good French into bad English for publication in *The Popular Tribune*, a dingy little five-column journal devoted to the glorification of the 'new philosophy of life.' And so on through the list." Another speaks of a "talented fresco-painter who was set to digging coal, at which employment he was able to make the magnificent sum of fifteen cents a day." But these remarks may be

155

somewhat misleading as to the general personnel of the colony. Only a few had been men of mark in France. Saint-Simonism had appealed to the highly intellectual classes, and so, to a less exclusive degree, had Fourierism; Icarianism had gone home to the *ouvrier* class,—the sturdy young tailors and shoe-makers and mechanics of the provincial towns all over France. But, none the less, they were a re-markable body of men. The very nature of their experiment had been a sifting process, had developed their intellects, and had made them men of thought and character.

The young architect referred to in the passage quoted above, was scarcely more than a lad when he joined the advance guard of Icarians who left Havre for Texas on Feb. 3, 1848. On reaching New Orleans and learning of the outbreak of the Revolu-tion in Paris, this young man, A. Picquenard by name, was in favor of returning to France; and abandoned the pioneer party. But with a young man's curiosity he determined to see Indians before returning home, and spent a year or two among the tribes in the Indian Territory. Meanwhile Icaria had become located at Nauvoo, and Picquenard there rejoined the society. His first large achievement as an American architect was to have been made in the completion of the great Mormon temple and its transformation into Icarian assembly-halls and school-rooms. Picquenard was absent on business connected with this building project when a great storm demolished the temple walls. He never returned, but took up his abode at St. Louis, where in later years he made a reputation as an architect second to none in the country. The two finest buildings in the West, the new State-houses of Illinois and Iowa, will for centuries be monuments to his genius. He died in 1876.[1]

There are several surviving members of the first band of Texas pioneers. One was too sick to follow his comrades away from Texas, and he remains to-day a flourishing citizen of Dallas. A few others are scattered through the west, at Nauvoo, at St. Louis, or in different Iowa towns. But while nearly all the old Icarians keep their faith in the principles of their youth and retain sympathy with the struggling little community, only one of the first advance guard remains an active Icarian. Alexis A. Marchand has been a prominent man from the first. He was the Secretary and Treasurer of the Texas party, a young man of such courage and devotion as only the spirit of '48 could have produced. He had been a student at Paris and a clerk in an attorney's office, and was regarded as having more literary ability than the young mechanics who surrounded him. At Nauvoo he was made useful in the work of education and especially in the busy

---

[1] More than one young and rising architect owes his success to association with Picquenard, among the number being Mr. M. E. Bell, the Supervising Architect of the United States Treasury Department.

printing-office. He was one of the leaders of the party which withstood Cabet, and he edited some very strong numbers of the *Revue Icarienne*, in justification of the action of the Nauvoo majority, for circulation in France after Cabet's withdrawal and death. In 1857 he was made president of the community, and was also the first president after the reorganization in Iowa two or three years later. Since that time he has repeatedly filled the presidential chair. He is now a man of benign and venerable aspect, but in full vigor of body and mind. No one can know him without being impressed with the purity, dignity, and unselfishness of his character. Serene and kindly in manner, lofty in his standards of right and duty, almost a mystic in his devotion to communism and the welfare of mankind, Marchand is a true type of the altruist. To have produced a few such characters as Marchand is itself enough to redeem Icarianism from the charge of utter failure. He was a prominent member of the party of the old people in the unhappy division of 1877, which not only cleft the community in twain, but also divided families,—his son, Alexis Marchand, going with the young party.

On a farm of five or six hundred acres adjoining the land of the New Icarian Community lives a a man who has made himself a part of Icarian history,—Jean Baptiste Gérard. In France he was a young cabinet-maker, of bright mind and remarkably strong characteristics. Though only twenty-five years old, he was the leader of the third advance guard, which left France in the fall of 1848 and met the retreating Texas pioneers at New Orleans. He became at Nauvoo a member of Cabet's administration, filling the office of Director-General of Finances. In the quarrel with Cabet he became the most prominent figure, and was made Cabet's successor in the presidential office in 1856. In 1857 he found it necessary to resign and retire temporarily from the society in order to act as assignee for the community. This duty occupied him a number of years, and to his honorable discharge of the trust were due the payment of the creditors on the one hand and the preservation of the society on the other. Many a long and weary journey on horseback or on foot did he make over the several hundred miles of almost uninhabited prairies between Nauvoo and western Iowa, in the prosecution of his unpaid task. In 1863 he had fully completed the duties of the trust and was about to re-enter the society (his withdrawal of course had only been technical); the community was not very rich nor prosperous, but it was on a safe footing and had fair prospects; Gérard had no other home, and his family had always remained in the community; what it retained of fortune he had a right to feel was due to him more than to any other man. But there was a prominent member with whom he was not in accord, and he feared that his return might endanger the harmony of the society. He was forty years of age, and had given the community fifteen years of talented and self-sacrificing service. With the pittance of twenty dollars apiece which the Icarian constitution at that time allowed to withdrawing members, he took his family and departed to find a new home. It is not apprehension of their own failure in the competitive struggle which impels such men as Gérard to seek community life. As we have said, he owns to-day a magnificent farm of several hundred acres; and he is surrounded by a phalanx of sturdy, manly sons who do him honor. Gérard has never lost his faith in communism, nor has his success made him a mere sordid money-getter. He has always remained a friend and adviser of the neighboring community, and has kept abreast of the social movements and thought of the day. In the Icarian quarrel of 1877 he espoused the cause of the old party, and published in their defence a tract entitled "Quelques Vérités sur la dernière Crise Icarienne." The Icarian split had attracted wide attention among French socialists both in this country and in Europe. Communistic bodies in New York, Chicago, St. Louis, Keokuk, and elsewhere, had endeavored to prevent the separation, and various French papers had published accounts favoring one party or the other. Under these circumstances Gérard constituted himself the cham-

pion of the old party, and in 1880 and 1881 published several numbers of a paper which he called
*L'Observateur.* This engaged in lively controversy
with *La Jeune Icarie*, the organ of the young branch,
and also contained valuable reminiscences of early
Icarian days. In this plain and simple-hearted old
French farmer on the Iowa prairies is the stuff from
which statesmen and generals are made. Force,
patience, sagacity, and a certain largeness of mind
and character mark him as one of nature's noble-
men.

The leader of the second advance guard was
P. J. Favard, whose letter from Texas to Cabet has
been quoted in a former chapter. In the Nauvoo
controversy Favard sided against Cabet, although
his brother-in-law. He soon after withdrew from
the society, and is to-day a merchant in Keokuk,
Iowa. Of the Cheltenham leaders, the young
lawyer Mercadier whom Cabet designed to be his
successor, and who was president at Cheltenham
for the first year, is now a gentleman of wealth and
influence in St. Louis. Charles Raynaud, who was
equally prominent in the Cheltenham movement, is,
with other ex-Icarians, resident in New York City.

There are some vigorous specimens of manhood
among the second generation, who have spent their
lives in Icaria;—for it must be remembered that
Icaria is more than a third of a century old. Eugene
F. Bettannier preferred to remain with the old

party.   He is a man whose good sense and shrewd intelligence would be recognized in any sphere of life.   His father, long since dead, was a leading man at Nauvoo.   Eugene Mourot and Emile Fugier were, from the first, chief agitators in the young people's movement.   Mourot was born in Paris, the son of E. Mourot, a revolutionist of '48, who was a victim of the bloody contest of the " bourgeois reaction " of June.   His young children were sent to America and brought up as Icarians.   Fugier is a native of Lyons, that cradle of revolution, and in early childhood accompanied his father to Nauvoo. Both Fugier and Mourot are men of energy and practical ability, and Icaria-Speranza will doubtless owe much to them.

Antoine von Gauvain, who died at Corning, Iowa, in January, 1883, was an Icarian of blessed memory.   Born in Berlin of a French Huguenot family, the son of an army officer, he became an army officer himself.   At twenty-five he came to America, edited a French paper in New York for a time, was a teacher in several different States, and at length joined Icaria at Nauvoo.   He served three years in the Union army and then reëntered the community.   He sided with the young party in the division ; but two years before his death he withdrew and made his home in Corning.   Gauvain was one of the most scholarly men ever in the community.   He was acquainted with languages, literature, philosophy, and history. His was a spirit so gentle and so guileless, though so brave and soldierly, that every one loved him. He was of noble blood and of still nobler nature.

The admission of six Internationalists to membership in Icaria in 1876 has been mentioned. Their careers and characters are of sufficient interest to have more particular attention. The six were: A. Sauva, Emile Peron, J. Laforgue, A. Tanguy, S. Dereure, and Charles Levy. Arsen Sauva is by trade a tailor. Of his early history I have learned nothing. In about 1860 he came from France to join the Cheltenham Icarians at St. Louis. He remained in that community until its dissolution, and then entered the Union army serving until the end of the war. He returned to France and fought through the Franco-Prussian war. He played an active and prominent part in the commune rising of 1871, being an officer and acquainted with all the leaders. After the collapse of the commune government he took refuge in this country. He was a member of the notable Congress of the International Society at the Hague in 1872, and aided in the expulsion of Bakounine and the Anarchist faction. Returning to this country and working at his trade in Chicago, St. Louis, and New York, he joined the Iowa Icarians in 1876, where he was soon elected to the presidency, and threw his influence with the Conservative party. Sauva is not a man of many words, but he has seen the world, and does his own thinking. Two pamphlets in my possession, "La Crise Icarienne" and "Icarie," prove that he is master of a brilliant and cogent French style, while the books in his humble home show him to be a student of the French social philosophers. The sincerity and thorough integrity of Sauva's character are manifest to all who know him. Since the bitter quarrel in which he and Peron were so active upon opposite sides, the two men have not been on terms of friendship. Yet even Peron bears the following high testimony as to Sauva's character : [1]

" I have so bitterly fought Sauva's course of action during Icarian troubles that one might expect me to write about him with a pen dipped in gall and aloes. Well, it would not be right ; for Sauva with all his shortcomings is certainly a high type of man. His errors, blunders, and mistakes, his straying judgment and reason on men and events, do not impair his faith and commendable devotion to principles that we claimed to be wrong but that he believed to be right. * * * If all social workers had his perseverance, endurance, devotedness, and moral courage, the world would soon adopt better modes of social relations. Sauva is a fine example of the faculty of altruism as discovered by A. Comte, for he can suffer, work, and live for others. Is not that very much in a man, especially in a country where the dollaromaniacal disease is so prevailing ? "

Emile Peron himself is a younger man, and has

---

[1] I take the liberty to quote from a private letter.

not so long a history. He too was engaged in the Paris Commune of 1871, and came to New York immediately after. He was a machinist by trade, but a philosopher, critic, and scholar, by natural instinct. In the workingmen's clubs of Paris, at night lectures, and in one way or another, he managed to find food for his voracious intelligence, and when he arrived at New York, though only a young proletarian of twenty-three or thereabouts, his scientific baggage was very considerable. It is not often, even among those trained from early boyhood in the best schools, that one finds a young man who is so conversant with philosophy, history, belles-lettres, political and social economy, and the natural sciences, as this Parisian mechanic. Quotations already given show that he has learned to write a very picturesque English. In philosophy he is an unqualified Positivist. If he does not fully sympathize with Anarchists and Nihilists, he can at least make a very apologetic statement of their doctrines. His keen critical faculty makes his conversation sparkling and epigrammatic. It is to be hoped that Icaria-Speranza may afford Peron time for systematic study and for literary work.

La Forgue and Levy follow their trades in Iowa towns, and seem to have lost somewhat of their pristine fervor for social reform, according to the report of their former brethren in Icaria. This is not the case with Tanguy and Dereure, both of

whom have returned to Paris. Tanguy is an accomplished fresco-painter. He was an active Communist in 1871, and was obliged to flee for his life,
first to England and then to America. After the
amnesty he left Icaria and resumed his old calling,
among the palaces and salons of the gay French
capital. But he plays his part in the work of social
agitation, and is known among the "militantes."
As for Simon Dereure, he is no ordinary man. He
was a member of the Commune Government of Paris
in 1871, and also with Sauva a member of the International Congress at the Hague in 1872. Dereure
is a shoemaker of superior skill; and while he shoes
the Paris plutocracy for a living, his real calling is
that of a social agitator. He is a man of force,
energy, and convictions,—one of the sort whom
revolutions bring to the front.

As has been said, the Leroux family constitute
the nucleus of the California colony. The name
Leroux is entitled to occupy a prominent place in
the history of modern French socialism. The two
brothers, Pierre and Jules Leroux, were among the
group of brilliant disciples of Saint-Simon. Pierre,
the elder of the two, had already made his reputation as a distinguished Parisian journalist, and in
1829 his paper, the *Globe*, was transformed into an
organ of Saint-Simonism.[1] After the breaking up
of Saint-Simonism into rival sects, Pierre Leroux

---

[1] For the part played by Pierre Leroux in the St.-Simonian movement, See Booth's "St.-Simon and St.-Simonism."

withdrew and became a socialistic philosopher on his own account. He founded the so-called Humanitarian School, the doctrines of which were of a rather mystical and transcendental character. He wrote many books, which at the time made a marked impression on the intellectual people of France. For years he was intimately associated with George Sand, and exerted upon her philosophical opinions an influence as strong as was that which afterward Mr. Lewes exercised upon those of George Eliot. Like most other dreamy philosophers, Pierre Leroux also indulged in the construction of an ideal society, which he named "Speranza." Jules Leroux, born in 1805, was seven years younger than his brother, and though also a man of ideas and of literary talents, he was not so prominent as Pierre, with whom he was intimately associated, and whose views in general he shared. Both brothers became Representatives in the Legislative Assembly after the Revolution of 1848, and both were exiled, victims of Louis Napoleon's *coup d'état* of December 2, 1851. They found homes in the island of Jersey, where for many years they maintained their families by agriculture. It was not a small mitigation of their hardships that in their exile they enjoyed the company of Victor Hugo. In 1869 Pierre Leroux returned to Paris, where he died in 1871. Jules Leroux resolved to make a home in America; and in 1867, with his family of now full-grown children,

he settled on government land in Kansas, where he
and his sons acquired homestead claims.  Here, in
1872, they were joined by Adam Dehay, who afterward married the youngest daughter of Jules Leroux.
Dehay was a young Frenchman who had seen life
in various parts of his native country, had spent
some years in London, and had come to America in
1866.  He bought the homestead of his father-in-
law, and undertook the formation of a community
thereon, but without success.  In 1877 Paul Leroux,
one of the sons, went to Iowa and joined the
Icarians, whither he was followed by his father and
mother, and afterward by his brothers and by Dehay.
The old hero of '48 lived for several years in the
Icarian community, but did not become a member.
He had begun in Kansas the publication of a little
French paper expository of his views on social and
religious philosophy, and continued its publication
in Iowa, and afterward in California up to his death
in October, 1883.  The last number of his paper,
" L' Etoile des Pauvres et des Souffrants," was completed a few days after his death by his son, Pierre
Leroux, and contained a touching account of the old
philosopher's life, doctrines, and  personal traits.
Jules Leroux was undoubtedly a man of pure and
noble character and of a strong religious nature.
His sons revere his memory and his opinions ; and it
is their desire to honor and perpetuate the associated
labors of their uncle and their father which has led

them to insist upon the retention of the name "Speranza" in the title of the community. Dehay must be regarded as the prime mover in the California enterprise. His purpose in joining Icaria had been to found a colony in a warmer climate after having gained some practical experience of community life. "Icaria-Speranza" may trace its lineage on the one side to Cabet, and on the other through the Leroux family to Saint-Simon.

The story of Emile Bée furnishes a rather characteristic Icarian biography. Bée was a tailor's son in northern France, and became a tailor himself. At the age of sixteen he went to Paris, where he found the tailors very active in the secret revolutionary society of Barbés and Blanqui, under which influences he became indoctrinated in Communism. He identified himself with the numerous disciples of Cabet, and subscribed of his humble means to aid the grand Icarian colonization. He was one of many thousands who were arrested on occasion of the *coup d'état* of Dec. 2, 1851, and he soon managed to leave France for the gold mines of California, where he spent some years. In 1862 he returned to France. As a member of the 69th Battalion of the National Guard, he was actively engaged in the defence of Paris in 1870, and in 1871 served the Commune. He found it expedient to return to California the same year, and became active in the San Francisco section of the International

Society. A few years later he joined Dehay and his friends in the purchase of the Cloverdale estate, and is now a peaceful citizen of Icaria-Speranza.

Such are a few hasty pen pictures of some of the men whose lives have been identified with Icaria. Many more, perhaps equally interesting and adventurous, might be given ; but these will suffice to show that French Communists are not necessarily the tremendous villains or the blood-thirsty wretches which we Americans are generally taught to believe that they are. Some of their doctrines may be dangerous to the existing order of society ; probably they are. History may render her final verdict in condemnation of many of their actions ; probably she will. But good men may mistake in their opinions and may honestly err in their actions ; and we can never understand the history and meaning of social movements in France, or in any other country, unless we render due credit to the sincerity, devotion, courageous self-denial, and grand enthusiasm for humanity, of many of the participants in those movements.

# XI.

## SOME KINDRED SOCIAL EXPERIMENTS.

# XI.

ONE cannot long explore the history of a social experiment like that of Icaria until he has discovered that the seeming isolation of the experiment is more apparent than real. He encounters threads of connection and lines of influence extending in most unexpected directions ; and if he follows those threads they will lead him into the labyrinths of a world of whose very existence, probably, he had been unaware. The past ten years have been full of earnest inquiry and discussion, in the larger circles of American society, touching all matters of social reform ; but the persons engaged in those discussions have been almost absolutely ignorant of the equally earnest efforts embodied in the obscure literatures and obscure social experiments which this same decade has produced in out-of-the-way nooks and crannies of nearly every State in the Union. There is no formal organization among these obscure experimenters and theorists ; their ideas are infinitely varied ; they are unlike in every thing except in their despair of the present structure of society, and also in this, that they have made

173

themselves peculiar by their views or their practices; and these two things supply a bond of loose federation.

These people constitute a little world within a world. The large world is not even aware of their existence; while they have the advantage of knowing their own world and also of knowing the great world perfectly well. This network, interwoven with all manner of curious, intersecting influences and lines of intercommunication, constitutes what we may term the Communistic World, for lack of a better designation. Viewed in the aggregate, it contains those persons whose convictions or whose traditions make them the foes of modern individualistic, competitive society. Its unity is of a negative rather than of a positive character. Each element of its membership is working in its own chosen way to compass the transformation of society.

It comes to the surface most prominently in such manifestations as those of the International Society and the Socialistic Labor Party; yet, in such active measures the Communistic World is never in agreement and union, and perhaps the organizations named might better be regarded as forming a connecting link, or a transitional stage, between the obscure Communistic World and the substratum of the larger society. Newspapers, travel, personal correspondence, are the means of communication in this unseen world. Yet, though their papers are numbered by the score, and are not printed on secret presses, nor designedly kept from the perusal of the larger society, few people have read any of them, or even know of their existence. If this seems a little strange at first, it is really not so strange after all. Ordinarily people are much more interested in what goes on in their own world than in the things which pertain to worlds beyond their own. It does not, therefore, necessarily brand a man as an ignoramus if he has never heard of *The Sociologist*, published at Adair Creek, in the mountains of East Tennessee; or of *The Communist*, published near Glen-Allen, Bollinger County, Missouri; or of the *Matrimonial Review*, which issues from Farmersville, Pennsylvania; or of *The Agnostic*, whose home is Dallas, Texas, or of fifty more reform sheets which now exist or have existed within half a dozen years. Nevertheless, to read these papers and to learn the personal history of those who publish them, is to enter a new and a very curious field of sociological inquiry.

In the last sixty years there have been hundreds of attempts at associative or communistic organizations in this country, all but a few of which failed in their very inception. Thousands of people have been engaged in these short-lived enterprises. What becomes of these people? Has their futile attempt freed them from illusive hopes and unattainable ideals? Have they been, as we should suppose,

completely cured ?   Generally not.   It was the testimony of the community at Brook Farm that :

"The life which we now lead, though to a superficial
observer surrounded with so many imperfections and embarrassments, is far superior to what we were ever able to
attain in common society.   There is a freedom from the
frivolities of fashion, from arbitrary restrictions, and from
the frenzy of competition.   *   *   *   There is a greater
variety of employments, a more constant demand for the
exertion of all the faculties, and a more exquisite pleasure
in effort, from the consciousness that we are laboring,
not for personal ends, but for a holy principle ; and even
the external sacrifices which the pioneers in every enterprise are obliged to make, are not without a certain romantic charm, which effectually prevents us from envying
the luxuries of Egypt, though we should be blessed with
neither the manna nor the quails which once cheered a
table in the desert."

Some such feeling as that seems to be permanently retained by almost all who have ever engaged
in community life.   It is a notable fact that many
of these people who have enlisted in what they
deem the work of human amelioration have their
wits wonderfully quickened thereby, while the one-
sidedness of their development tends to deepen and
confirm opinions once received.   The ill-fated colonies of Robert Owen had passed into the history of
" extinct socialisms " a generation ago ; and yet the
writer hereof might designate one and another and

another of the now venerable associates of Owen, still fresh with enthusiasm and warm with sympathy for every proposed social reform. The last of the Fourierist Phalansteries disappeared before the war; but many of the men who were engaged in them may still be found wrestling with the problems of coöperation, or pounding away at something more radical. Icaria once numbered its hundreds of disciples. Most of them have disappeared, seemingly swallowed up in the mass of American society; but if the truth could be ascertained they would, in all probability, still be found to be communists at heart.

One would not unnaturally suppose that the attempts to form new communities would be made by new men who had not experienced the almost insuperable difficulties of such an enterprise. The fact is that the new propositions almost always come from men who have had abundance of disheartening experience, but who have a limitless stock of hope and faith. Widely different as are the American communities in point of origin, objects, and policy, there is still a strong sympathy among them all. Thus I found that a leading member of the Oneida Perfectionists was regarded as a friend and counsellor by the Icarians, widely divergent as were their religious views. I made the acquaintance at Icaria of an Ohio Shaker, who is in the habit of paying long and welcome visits to the French

materialists of Iowa. I found the Icarian women
clad in calicoes manufactured by the prosperous
German community known as the "Amana Inspirationists"; and I found that friendly correspondence
and acts of courtesy brought Icaria into relations
with various other communistic enterprises.

One of these, with which Icaria has a peculiarly
intimate relation, is the new colony known as the
"Mutual Aid Community," located at Glen-Allen, in
Bollinger County, Missouri, a hundred miles or more
below St. Louis, on the Iron Mountain Railroad.
Its actual working existence began only in the summer of 1883, and it has as yet only twenty or thirty
members, with a small capital. Its principles and
organization are essentially Icarian, though its members are Americans. Its founder is Mr. Alcander
Longley, who in 1867 was a member of Icaria. The
story of Mr. Longley's career is one so typical
of a certain class of American social reformers that
I shall give its outlines. Mr. Longley comes very
honestly by his advanced views. His father, who
was a Universalist minister at Cincinnati, took
a leading part in about 1843 in forming the Cler
mont (Ohio) Phalanx, which however lived only
three years. The Fourier movement was at its
height in those days and young Longley heard of
little else in his boyhood. At eighteen he proposed
to found a Phalanx himself, but without success;
at twenty-one, in the year 1853, he found himself a

member of the famous North American Phalanx, which was " the test-experiment on which Fourierism practically staked its all in this country."[1] Horace Greeley was its Vice-President, Charles Sears was its practical chief, and Albert Brisbane was its sponsor. Longley did not remain here many years, for in 1857 we find him undertaking to establish a Phalanx at Moore's Hill, Indiana. In 1864 he appears at Black Lake, Michigan, as the founder of a Coöperative Association. No failure could suppress Longley. In 1865 he is founding another Association at Foster's Crossing, Ohio. The year 1867 finds him and his family converted from the complicated system of Fourierism to a belief in Communism pure and simple, and admitted to membership in Icaria. But it did not suit Longley's temperament to be a quiet Icarian farmer ; he was born to be an apostle. So in 1868 he withdrew, went to St. Louis, founded his paper *The Communist* (which he has published ever since), and advertised his purpose to establish a community on Icarian principles. So came into being the " Reunion Community" in southwestern Missouri, in the county of Jasper. In the spring of 1870 "Reunion" had twenty-seven members, among them being several remarkably intelligent men, and the prospects of the establishment were counted good.

---

[1] The story of the North American Phalanx is best told by J. H. Noyes in his " History of American Socialisms," pp. 449 to 512.

But suddenly the enterprise collapsed. Longley had good old-fashioned views about marriage, while some of his companions were inclined to the doctrines of free-love; and on this rock "Reunion" split. Mr. Longley returned to St. Louis in the best of spirits, and *The Communist* began to publish an extended prospectus of the "Friendship Community" which Mr. Longley proposed to establish in Dallas County, Missouri, near the town of Buffalo. In 1872 "Friendship Community" was an actuality. Its ups and downs, hopes and possibilities, were food for the issues of *The Communist* for a period of five years. "Friendship" never attained a large membership or a strong financial footing. It did not win the favor of the stalwart Missourians of Dallas County, who regarded it as something essentially equivalent to Mormonism, and a disgrace to good Missouri society. Accordingly they organized a "Committee," and Mr. Longley was warned that his institution must go. Means were taken to give emphasis to the warning. So the "Friendship Community" closed business in 1877.

Again Mr. Longley returned to St. Louis. This was the year of strikes, riots, labor unions, and socialistic political organizations. Mr. Longley's paper became, temporarily, an organ of the socialistic labor party. Meanwhile he published the prospectus of a "Liberal Community," to be organized in St. Louis. This community never existed except in prospectus. In 1879 we find *The Communist* published at Cincinnati, energetically proposing to revive the " Friendship Community," and meanwhile giving much attention to politics and the state of the country. Two years pass and *The Communist* in 1881 is issued from the " Principia Community," Polk County, Missouri, in which community Mr. Longley has now become a social pillar. His sojourn in " Principia " is brief ; for in January, 1882, we find him once more domiciled at St. Louis and advertising to the world the doctrines and prospects of the "Mutual Aid Community," which he desired to found at Glen-Allen, Bollinger County, Missouri. " Mutual Aid," though a humble and small outfit, became a resident fact in Bollinger County in July, 1883. To predict that it will live long and prosper would be the very climax of reck- lessness after the history we have just narrated ; though it is right to say that the " Mutual Aid " has some reasons for regarding itself as on a more solid basis than its predecessors. As for Mr. Longley himself, he is doubtless a gentleman of good conscience, of complete faith in communism, and of such buoyant spirit and fine pluck that he never acknowledges himself beaten. His paper has been an organ for other enterprises besides his own, and its files are a storehouse of information con- cerning the crude and obscure communistic enter- prises of the West during fifteen years past. A

hobby with Mr. Longley is inter-communal organization. He advocates a loose union, or at least
an occasional delegate convention of all the communities in the United States for the furtherance
of such views and ends as they have in common.
From such a beginning he pictures the gradual
transformation of the whole country into a congeries
of united communities.

One of the most remarkable men associated with
Mr. Longley in the " Reunion Community " was
William Frey. Though never an Icarian, he has
visited Icaria, and through association with Mr.
Longley he may be regarded as having gained some
of his afflatus from our little French centre of influence. Frey is a Russian, and was an astronomer
in the service of his government, with a brilliant
career before him. But his communistic views subjected him to political persecution, and he came to
America in 1868. In the spring of 1870 he went
west, and entered Mr. Longley's " Reunion Community " with his family. After the collapse of that
enterprise we find him, with another of its recent
members, on government land in Howard County,
Kansas, proposing to found there the " Progressive
Community." There he remained for several years,
publishing a paper called *The Progressive Communist*,
and endeavoring to found a colony on hygienic and
high moral principles. It had neither length of days
nor temporary success. For several years following

that effort, I do not know his history, though from
the recent appearance in Boston of a little book entitled " The Religion of Humanity," I infer that he
must have spent much time in thought and study.
With a profoundly philosophical mind, and at the
same time a deeply religious nature, Mr. Frey adopts
and expounds the religion of Positivism with the
moral earnestness of an apostle.   He is at present
engaged in a most interesting work.   In Douglas
County, Oregon, a company of thirty young Russians
founded the " New Odessa Community " in the fall
of 1882.   They had great confidence in Mr. Frey,
and asked him to live with them and be their teacher
and guide in the theory and practice of Communism.
They have seven hundred acres of land, and their
material prospects are not bad.   But Mr. Frey is not
chiefly concerned to win a material success.   As he
says in a letter to the writer : " I am convinced that
a proper communal life must be a school for moral
improvement, a coöperation for mutual assistance
and support in realization of the common ideal of a
better life; that, in short, moral aims must pre-
dominate over material."   Mr. Frey is fully convinced that no bond except religion can permanently
unite men in communistic societies, and he is undertaking the ethical culture of these young countrymen of his as the only means of saving their enterprise.   How he is succeeding may be seen from the
following sentences which I extract from a private
letter written by an intelligent observer :

"I find the thirty Russians full of good feeling ; they embrace each other each day like devoted brothers and sisters. Every act of their social life is dominated by the ideas of conduct imposed upon them by the teaching and personal magnetism of Frey. Frey's idea of happiness is to eat two meals a day of crackers and raw fruit, to touch no kind of stimulant, to do all the labor between meals so as to be free after to study,—the evenings in his community to be devoted to study and moral and social exhortations in which all should join. This includes personal criticism with the purpose of perfecting character. In the morning there is music and singing, which exercise is supposed to make those who join in it feel more friendly to each other, so that if you meet one of them before the music he hurries by with a cold "good morning" ; but if you meet him afterward he warmly shakes your hand and kisses you. As a friend of Frey's I am both surprised and delighted at the success he has made. The disciples are all young and full of devotion ; it is charming to see such persons, resolved to love each other, and determined to do what is right. It is unquestionable that these persons have given up bad habits for a social purpose, led to do so not by superstition, but by a rational conception of personal and public duty. For instance, they were nearly all smokers, and without exception have given up the habit as unwholesome and unsocial. * * * It is a charming spot amongst the mountains which these Russians have secured. I like the people very much indeed, and believe they will be successful in establishing such a society as they aim at."

Mr. Longley in Missouri, and Mr. Frey in Oregon,

are instances of what one may discover by following
the threads he finds radiating from such a centre as
" Icaria " ; just as he would have discovered
" Icaria " if his point of departure had been the
" Mutual Aid," or just as he would have found the
" Mutual Aid " and " Icaria " if his investigation
had begun at " New Odessa." Almost equally
striking is the story of N. T. Roumain, an associate
of Longley at one time, and an applicant for admission to Icaria at another time, who, in 1877,
founded the " Esperanza Community " in Kansas,
—an enterprise which had its bright day, but ended
in sadness and disaster. Or one might make a long
tale of the adventures of Earl Joslin, who was
Longley's associate in his earliest attempts at Phalansteries, who has since been in various enterprises,
and who, at last accounts, was endeavoring to organize a " Coöperative Association " in Rice
County, Kansas. Though these sketches might be
multiplied, it is not my object to give a catalogue
of abortive attempts at association, but rather
merely to suggest the curious ramification into
which an apparently isolated social experiment is
likely to widen before the investigator, and to call
attention to a kind of sociological study deserving
of more consideration than it has received.

Beginning with a single community and with no
object of studying American communities in general,
I have incidentally discovered and could enumerate

probably not fewer than fifty distinct attempts to found communistic or semi-communistic associations in the United States since 1870. Most of them were obscure, fruitless, and ephemeral. They attracted almost no public attention, and some of them were perhaps worthy of very little. If they had been in Europe, they would doubtless have thriven on the persecution of government and the calumnies of the press, and such opposition would have cemented and preserved them ; while in this country their very liberty to be or not to be, to become incorporated, to buy and sell and get gain, to wear peculiar garments, to preach peculiar doctrines, and to worship strange gods, has been a centrifugal force that community bonds have seldom been able to stand against.

# XII.

## APPENDIX.

# APPENDIX I.

## CONTRACT OF THE NEW ICARIAN COMMUNITY
### OF ADAMS COUNTY, IOWA.

IN order to form an association whose object is the realization of Community on Icarian principles, and the formation and establishment of a common fund for the assurance to each of us and of our children of our wants, intellectual and material, in all conditions of life—infancy, old age, health, sickness, and infirmity,—and being resolved to give to our association a solid basis and to place its existence beyond the risk of all misunderstanding and of all controversy which might arise among us,—

We, the undersigned, members of the ex-Community Icarian of Adams County, Iowa, do freely and voluntarily make, admit, sign, and accept this contract for the formation of an association which shall be known under the name of the New Icarian Community of Adams County, Iowa.

Consequently we give and transfer freely to our said association all property of every nature and of every kind immovable, movable, and mixed—which we have and possess now, and also all property of every kind which we may acquire in the future—by inheritance, gift, or otherwise, to be during our lives and after our death and for ever the exclusive property of the New Icarian Community.

We promise and agree freely and formally that, at no time and in no case will we, or any of us, make any reclamation or demand, nor will we claim any pecuniary compensation for any property which we give now or which we may give in the future to our association, either for interest or for capital, for work, labor, or any other service which we may have performed for it.

We formally enjoin upon our heirs and upon their guardians, in perpetual succession, not to make any reclamation against our said

association for any thing which we have freely and voluntarily given
to it.

We consent to submit our children during their minority to the
care and the absolute control of our association, giving it the same
rights and the same powers over them, and charging it with the same
duties toward them, as if they were under its guardianship conformably with the laws of Iowa.

We, who sign this contract, engage ourselves and enjoin upon our
heirs, and upon their executors, administrators, and guardians, never
to bring any suit in law or in equity against our said association,
neither to recover any property which we have freely and voluntarily
given to it, nor to obtain any salary or pecuniary compensation for
labor or service done or rendered by us or them for the said society.

We engage ourselves to give all our time, all our strength, and all
our capacities for the service of the association, during all the time
while we are members of it, and at every time and under all circumstances without opposition or murmur to obey the laws and regulations which shall be adopted conformably to this contract, and to the
following articles :

ARTICLE 1.—The place of business of the New Icarian Community for the present, and until it may be changed, shall be Icaria,
Adams County, Iowa ; the nature of the business, which shall com-
mence on the first of May, 1879, shall be : agriculture, horticulture,
industry, art, commerce, mills, and manufactures.

ART. 2.—This association shall last for ninety-nine years, and shall
not be dissolved before that time for any reason whatsoever, without
the unanimous consent of all the adult members.

ART. 3.—The capital or the property of the New Icarian Community shall consist of all which the founders may have recovered, in immovable or movable property in the liquidation of the former Icarian
Community, dissolved by a judgment of the Court of Adams County,
Iowa, rendered the 17th of August, 1878 ; and of all the increase re-
sulting from the operations of the agriculture, horticulture, mills,
manufactures, commerce, and arts of the said society, of all gifts
made by strangers, and of all money paid, or property given by new
members when they have been admitted to final membership.

Art. 4.—The social capital shall be common and indivisible. It shall be recorded in the name of the New Icarian Community.

Art. 5.—The affairs of this society shall be conducted and administered by five directors, chosen among the members, as follows a President, a Secretary-Treasurer, a Director of Industry, a Director of Agriculture, a Director of Clothing. Each director shall hold office for a year, and shall be elected separately in a general assembly, which shall meet on the 3d of February of every year after the year 1879 for this especial purpose.

Art. 6.—No member of the association who has not reached the age of twenty-five years at least shall be eligible to the office of director, and no one shall be eligible to the presidency who is not at least thirty years old and has not been a member of the society for at least five years. The founders of the society are excepted from this rule. No member shall be chosen director more than twice consecutively, and after a member shall have been elected director twice consecutively, he shall not be re-elected director until after having been a year out of office.

Art. 7.—The title of all the fixed property which the society now possesses, or which may hereafter be acquired, is and shall be vested in the name of the five directors hereinafter named, or of their successors in office, for the use and benefit of the said association ; and may be sold, conveyed, or mortgaged by a vote of the association as hereinafter described, and the five directors shall sign and acknowledge all the conveyances, and set upon them the seal of the association.

Art. 8.—In all transactions relating to movable property, the President of the community alone may buy, sell, and contract in the name of the community, after authorization of the general assembly. Every contract, sale, or purchase which has not been made by the President, or upon an order written and signed by him, shall not in any manner bind the association. If by any reason not provided for in this contract, it is impossible for the President to attend to the affairs of the society, the other directors shall appoint one of their members to act temporarily in his place.

Art. 9.—The directors of this association are responsible before the general assembly, and can be suspended or removed from their office by a vote of the majority of the male members. In case of the death, suspension, dismissal, withdrawal, or expulsion of a member of the administration, the assembly shall fill the vacancy eight days after either the death, suspension, dismissal, withdrawal, or expulsion of a member.

ART. 10.—Every business transaction exceeding in amount $100, must be signed by the President and the Secretary, and must bear the seal of the society in order to be binding.

ART. 11.—All male adult members who have been definitely admitted, are eligible to all the offices of the society subject to Article 7 of this contract, and will participate by their vote in all decisions. The adult members of the "sexe féminin" have the right to vote upon all admissions and exclusions ; they are both electors and eligible for all committees and for the office of the Director of Clothing. They have the right to vote upon the revision of this contract, upon the dissolution of the society, and in general upon all matters of moral and intellectual interest, such as education, propaganda, and amusements. Minors and members admitted on probation have no right to vote in any case.

ART. 12.—The suffrage shall be exercised in the general assembly and in person ; no vote by proxy or substitute will be permitted. The vote in general assembly may be taken in any manner whatsoever, except in the following cases : admissions, exclusions, and the election of the Board of Directors, which votes shall be by written ballot, signed or unsigned at the will of the voter.

ART. 13.—Provisional admissions and definitive admissions shall take place in general assembly by a vote of at least nine tenths of the members having the right to vote. Adult candidates, when they are admitted definitively, shall pay $100 ; minors, $20. They shall conform to all the special law on the subject of admission. Provisional admission must take place, at the latest, fourteen days after the arrival of the candidate at Icaria ; six months after arrival, a second vote likewise is necessary for permission to continue the novitiate. Definitive or full admission shall take place one year after the provisional admission. Any admission not made conformably to the terms of this contract is null and void, and does not confer any right.

ART. 14.—When a candidate has not the means to pay a part or all of the sum required by Article 13, the society may exempt him by a vote of nine tenths of the voting members.

ART. 15.—No stranger may reside more than fourteen days in the association without the consent of nine tenths of the members having right to vote.

ART. 16.—The adults and minors admitted provisionally are held to obey the directors and to perform the labor assigned to them by decision of the assembly general. They shall labor at all times according to their strength and their capacity, and shall receive in compensation for their labor, proportionally to their needs and to the means of the society, their lodging, food, clothing, care in sickness, attention and care for the children and the aged ; but no other compensation of any sort.

ART. 17.—Minors who have lost father and mother in the association, shall be supported and shall remain under the surveillance of the society, which shall take the same care of them and give them the same support as the children whose parents are living. When the minors, having arrived at their majority, desire to remain in the association, they shall state the same in writing to the general assembly, and shall sign this contract. They shall then have all the rights of members admitted definitively by this contract.

ART. 18.—The principal object of this association in conducting the affairs described and considered in these articles, being that of creating and establishing a fund which shall provide for the needs and comforts of the young, the old, the sick, and the infirm, no dividend shall be paid to any member ; but every accumulation of wealth shall be added to the common fund.

ART. 19.—Every member who has decided to retire from the society shall give to the general assembly fifteen days' notice in writing. Every member retiring in this manner shall receive from the society the pledge of a gift of $100 if he be an adult, and $20 if he be a minor. This amount may be increased by a vote of three fourths of the general assembly, in the meeting which is held on the 3d of

February, for the election of the Board of Directors, upon the proposition of five members of the society.[1]

ART. 20.—The sale of annual products may be made when it is authorized by a vote of the majority of the adult men present in the general assembly, and the majority may decide upon the use and the disposition of such products and of the proceeds of their sale. Besides these annual revenues of the society, the majority may—but not more than once in a month—decide upon the use or the disposition of a portion of the social capital not to exceed $100. Every disposition of the social capital beyond the amount of $100, must be made by a vote of nine tenths of the voting members, and the disposition of the fifth part of the social capital may not be made except by the unanimous consent of the members voting.

ART. 21.—This association does not approve the borrowing of money as a general rule ; but as it may sometimes be necessary, the President may, by a vote of the general assembly, borrow money to the amount of $100, when the loan does not require mortgage ; but this may be done only once a month.

ART. 22.—No loan under any other conditions shall bind the society, unless by the consent of nine tenths of the voting members.

ART. 23.—All the ordinary affairs of the society shall be conducted and decided by a majority vote of the adult men who are present in the general assembly at the moment of the vote, except in cases specified and provided for in the other articles of this contract.

ART. 24.—The general assembly of this association shall be composed of the members having the right to vote ; and its decisions shall bind the association when the half plus one of the men having the right to vote are present at the meeting. In case of urgency recognized by the majority of the men having the right to vote, that majority shall suffice to authorize the assembly to make decisions which shall bind the society when the postponement of a decision might be prejudicial to the interests of the society.

---

[1] *Note to Art.* 19.—This article was revised at the meeting of Feb. 3, 1883. Under the new rule, a man when admitted simply gives the society whatever he possesses. If he retires, he receives two thirds the amount of his initial deposit, and $25 additional for each year he has served the society. This rule applies to charter members and later admissions equally.

Art. 25.—Any member of this association may be expelled by a vote of nine tenths of the members having the right to vote, when that member has been guilty of voluntary disobedience, without any good reason, and of refusing repeatedly to perform the orders of the directors, or when he refuses to conform to the decisions of the general assembly, if, by his conduct, the said delinquent member has seriously prejudiced the moral and material interests of the society. The expulsion will take place in a special assembly called for that purpose, of which assembly and of the charges preferred against him the said member shall have fifteen days' notice. The member accused shall have every guaranty for the proof of his innocence and for the explanation of the acts of which he is accused. In case of withdrawal or expulsion from the society of a member who is the head of a family, that withdrawal or expulsion shall imply the withdrawal of his children under the age of fifteen years.

Art. 26.—If one or more members of this association shall rebel against its authority, or form a party detached from the common group, in the matter of *nourriture* (eating), of labor, of purchase and of sale, of loans and of gifts, or in any other manner ; or shall undertake to turn the society from its true end as specified above ; or shall leave the society for more than three consecutive days without the consent of a majority of three fourths of the members ; or shall labor repeatedly outside the community, or within its limits, for strangers, without the knowledge and consent of the assembly, that member or those members may be expelled by a majority of the members having the right to vote, but the member or members expelled shall have the right to receive the gift of $100 upon their expulsion, like members withdrawing. The member or members accused of offences against this contract shall not have the right to vote upon the penalty which shall be inflicted upon them by the assembly.

Art. 27.—All the laws and regulations necessary to execute and to carry into proper effect the objects of this association, provided they are not inconsistent with or opposed to this contract, may be made by a majority of the men.

Art. 28.—Five members of the association may, at every annual assembly for the election of the directors, propose the revision of any part of this contract whatsoever, and if a majority of nine tenths of the members having the right to vote, vote in favor of the proposed revision, it shall be placed upon the order of the day of the general assembly, discussed and voted upon three months after its presentation, and if at this last vote the nine tenths of the members having the right to vote decide in favor of such revision, it shall have full force and effect as part of this contract.

ART. 29.—In case of the dissolution of this association by the unanimous consent of all its members, or by any other unforeseen cause, the social capital and the property shall be divided as follows : First, all the debts or claims due or belonging to persons outside the society shall be determined and paid. Second, the members who were founders or who signed this contract at the date of its adoption, viz., May 1, 1879, shall receive, and shall be paid in money or in equivalent property the amount placed in the common fund by them at the date of the signature of this contract, or at any other later date, as the books of the association shall make evident. Third, the members who were not founders shall also receive in money or in equivalent property that which they have placed in the common fund of the association at the time of their definitive admission, or at any other time thereafter, as the books of the association may show. Fourth, the remainder of the property of the association, if there be any, shall be divided among the members according to the years of service of each adult member, reckoning from the time of his signature of this contract. Every adult member shall receive a part proportioned to his time of service under this contract. The period of service of the founders shall be counted, in reckoning their years of service, from the date of this contract ; the period of the other members shall be counted from their definitive admission ; the time of children born in the community, and of those who enter as minors, shall be counted from the day when they have attained their majority ; minor orphans shall have the right to ten years of service in making this division of the property in case of dissolution.

We, the undersigned, in full possession of our faculties intellectual and moral, knowing well and comprehending perfectly the above contract and all its articles, do adopt and accept them freely and voluntarily, and do engage ourselves not to make any reclamation of any sort or nature whatsoever against our said association which would not be in accordance with the terms of this contract.

The directors chosen conformably to this contract, in 1879, for the year 1879, to remain in office until Feb. 3, 1880, are as follows : E. F. Bettannier, President ; A. A. Marchand, Secretary-Treasurer ; V. E. Caillé, Director of Agriculture ; Armel Marchand, Director of Industry ; and Marie V. Marchand, Director of Clothing.

[Here follow signatures, acknowledged before a notary public, and the minute of the county recorder.]

# APPENDIX II.

## LAW UPON WITHDRAWAL AND EXPULSION FROM THE ICARIAN COMMUNITY.[1]

### SECTION I.—*Preamble.*

When a person has resolved to live in communism, and has made his demand for admission into Icaria, the greatest prudence, the most serious reflection, should be exercised in the accomplishment of the act, which, by its good or bad results may be classed among the most important acts of his life.

No inconsiderate enthusiasm for the beauty of the Icarian system should influence his mind, nor have weight in his decision. It is important that he separate from the causes of his determination all sentimentalism, all enthusiasm of a nature to conceal the truth from his eyes and make him conceive of the community as much more beautiful, more developed, more perfect than it really is, and its members better than they really are.

In the distance defects are unperceived, forms harmonize, all is embellished ; men are exalted in their merit, and things appear more beautiful than they are.

But if it is necessary that one should always be on his guard against mirages and illusions, it is especially important that he should do so in reference to an act which may result, in the future, in regrets to all concerned.

Icaria does not escape the rule of illusions ! The experience of many years demonstrates, on the contrary, that the hope of ameliorating his situation, the idea which he generally forms of Icaria and Icarians, the joy that he experiences in the thought of being able to live according to his principles, exercises over every distant candidate an irresistible enchantment, which in many cases suffices to conceal

---

[1] See page 131

from him the inconveniences of our society of equality, and leave on his mind only a conception of its advantages.

To these natural inclinations toward the transports of enthusiasm are added the great influence of the writings of Cabet, picturing the splendors that communism shall one day realize, and also the favorable impression that the regular publication of LA JEUNE ICARIE cannot fail to exercise over the mind, by its exposition of the organization, the principles, and the grandeur of the end which the community proposes to itself.

But in all things—it is necessary to repeat—it is a long distance from the desire to the realization, from the principle to the fact, from the theory to the practical embodiment ; and what is true elsewhere is true also in Icaria. Those who desire to join it ought to be thoroughly impressed with this fact, and act only after having thoroughly considered the gravity of the situation.

For, let us not forget, enthusiasm is ephemeral ! When its inspiration has passed, deceptions, discouragement, succeed to the enchantment, and a prompt return to individualism is often the sad consequence of it.

———

Theoretically, quitting old society to embrace the communistic life should be an irrevocable act. Those who join themselves to the community should do it for all time ; and whatever property they possess should be deposited in the social fund without power of recall. For if it is reasonable that one should withdraw himself from the iniquities of individualism, to adopt a better form of association, there can be no reason for quitting the latter in order to live again under the yoke of laws which one has once rejected with all his convictions.

Change for the better is logical ; returning upon one's steps, in the path of progress, is an absurdity.

Moreover, withdrawal often involves a multitude of inconveniences for the society and the seceders.

In what concerns the definite deposit of property there is, in fact, a certain inequality in this respect, that one family can retain some rights over a deposit while others have nothing which belongs to themselves.

It is true that the inequality reäppears only on the morrow of their departure. While persons live in Icaria equality is perfect as regards possession. But for the communists this difference with the seceders is not less an evil, which the financial weakness of Icaria can alone justify.

Later, when the community shall have grown, when its production shall be better assured and its general situation prosperous, it will be able, while giving increased comforts to its members, to exact guarantees of stability, and to establish equality even in the case of withdrawing members.

Meanwhile many inconveniences would result from holding too rigorously to principles deduced from pure reason, and upon this point, as upon others, it is necessary to conform to the exigencies of practical life.

Nevertheless, the sincere and firm intention to remain permanently in Icaria should be the basis of the application of every candidate.

But since the weakness and variableness of men compel us to anticipate withdrawals, and since, on the other hand, a member may so disregard his duties that the Society will feel itself under obligation to exclude him, it is important to regulate in advance, in the interest of seceders and of the Society, the condition which shall govern voluntary or constrained withdrawals.

### Section II.— *Withdrawal.*

ARTICLE 1.—Every member, provisional or absolute, can at any time, by giving notice to the delegates one month in advance, withdraw from the Community.

ART. 2.—The withdrawing member shall give notice of his purpose in a written paper or letter of withdrawal.

ART. 3.—The withdrawing member shall not be relieved of his duties until the Assembly shall have passed a vote accepting his resignation of membership.

### Section III.— *Withdrawal in the Novitiate.*

ART. 4.—When a provisional member shall decide to withdraw, the money, deeds, jewelry, credits, tools, and other things that he may have deposited on entering, with the knowledge of the trustees, shall be returned to him.

ART. 5.—The provisional member, being considered in every thing save voting a full member, no interest, rent, or revenue whatsoever, be it in money or in commodities which shall have been obtained by money, the credits or the property that he shall have deposited upon entrance, shall be returned to him. The revenue in all its forms belongs to the community.

## SECTION IV.— *Withdrawal of Full Members.*

ART. 6.—After having accepted the resignation of a full member, the General Assembly shall take into consideration the time that said member has passed in the community, the services that he has rendered to it, the value of his deposit, the condition of his family, his personal resources, and allow to him, under the title of gift, such sum of money or such property as the financial condition and interest of the community, being well considered, shall at the time permit it to give.

ART. 7.—The withdrawal of the husband involves the withdrawal of the wife, and *vice versâ ;* also the withdrawal of their children under twenty years of age. By a two-thirds vote the latter may be re-admitted upon their application.

## SECTION V.—*Cash Deposits.*

ART. 8.—When a member who has deposited in the common treasury more than a hundred dollars shall have offered his resignation of membership, the general assembly shall designate the times and the successive payments in the refunding of such deposit.

ART. 9.—Deposits not exceeding one hundred dollars shall be refunded within one year after the withdrawal of the depositor.

ART. 10.—The same amount shall be refunded that was deposited ; that is, it shall be refunded without interest.

ART. 11.—Likewise, after the dismissal of a member, the sums which the community shall refund to him in partial payments, by the direction of the general assembly, shall not bear interest. The exact amount contributed shall be refunded.

Art. 12.—Articles 8, 9, 11 shall be in force until the present debt of the community is paid.

Art. 13.—After that the General Assembly shall have the power to determine in advance the sums which shall be refunded yearly in case of withdrawal.

### Section VI.—*Deposits other than in Cash.*

Art. 14.—When a member shall contribute to the community a deposit other than cash, such as houses, lands, credits, mortgages, horses, cattle, etc., the said deposit, with a statement of its character, shall be recorded to the credit of the member on the books of the community.

Art. 15.—In case of withdrawal this deposit shall in the course of six months be returned to him in the condition in which it shall be at the time.

Art. 16.—When the community shall have sold a part or the whole of the lands, houses, or property of any kind, deposited by a member, the net product of this sale shall be placed to the account of said depositor, and he shall be reimbursed just as though his deposit had been made in ready money.

Art. 17.—The tools, arms, instruments, machines, books, furniture, etc., shall be returned immediately and in the condition in which they are at the time of withdrawal.

Art. 18.—No damage or indemnity shall be accorded for tools, instruments, or property of any kind, which shall have been mislaid, used, damaged, or destroyed.

### Section VII.—*Special Contracts.*

Art. 19.—When a candidate shall possess considerable money, and the conditions of the present law shall prevent his admission, the community may make a special contract with him respecting the manner in which his capital shall be refunded in case of his withdrawal.

Art. 20.—Nevertheless this special contract shall not be in opposition to Article 10, concerning the non-payment of interest for time anterior to withdrawal.

Art. 21.—Special contracts shall be recorded upon the books of the community at the pages devoted to the contracting persons, and signed by the latter and two trustees.

## Section VIII.—*Expulsion.*

Art. 22.—When a member shall not wish to conform to the laws ; when he shall refuse to fulfil his duties ; when he shall conduct himself improperly toward his associates ; when his general attitude shall constitute a real danger to the society, he can be expelled by a vote of two thirds of the members.

Art. 23.—This expulsion can only take place when the accused has been notified of the misdemeanors charged against him ten days in advance of the day for their investigation, and he shall have been given full liberty to defend himself before the assembly.

Art. 24.—As in admission so in dismission, the expulsion of the husband implies the withdrawal of his wife, and reciprocally ; also the withdrawal of their children under twenty years of age.

Art. 25.—Expelled members shall be settled with in accordance with the law upon withdrawals, as in the case of dismissed members.

## Section IX.—*Revision.*

Art. 26.—The present law is subject to annual revision beginning from the 1st of May, 1879, by a majority of two thirds of the members of the General Assembly.

———

This law was unanimously approved by the General Assembly Dec. 8, 1879.

# APPENDIX III.

## CONTRACT AND ARTICLES OF AGREEMENT OF THE ICARIA–SPERANZA COMMUNE.[1]

### SECTION I.—*Society.*

ARTICLE 1.—Know all men by these presents that we : Armand Dehay, Marie Dehay, Paul Leroux, Francoise Leroux, Pierre Leroux, Josephine Leroux, Gustave Provost, Irma Provost, Emile Bée, Caroline Bée, Eugene Mourot, Marie Mourot, Emile Fugier, Emilie Fugier, Therese James, Michel Brumme, Alexis Marchand, Louise Mourot,Louise Peron, Emile Peron,

and all others who shall be admitted and allowed to sign this Contract and Articles of Agreement ; being of age and in full knowledge of our action and deed, do hereby associate and form a society, under such name and conditions, and for such business and object as is hereinafter described.

ART. 2.—The name of this society is

### ICARIA–SPERANZA COMMUNE ;

and its location and principal place of business is on Bluxome Rancho, near Cloverdale, Sonoma County, State of California.

### SECTION II.—*General Object.*

ART. 3.—The general purpose of the Icaria-Speranza commune is as follows, to wit :

*A.*  To establish for humanity as an example and in devotion to its welfare, a system of society capable of rendering it happy.

*B.*  To prove to our fellow-men that community, based on solidarity, is realizable and possible.

---

[1] See page 145

*C.* To perform such labor, and use such sums of money, from time to time, as the commune may deem sufficient in publishing, advertising, and circulating the business and principles of the Icaria-Speranza Commune; but the aggregate of sums of money and reasonable value of labor applied to such advertising shall at no time be less than fifty dollars per annum.

*D.* To create a common fund, composed of money, real estate, personal property, and all kinds of other property, said common fund to be used for the mutual support and in the interest of all members composing this society; for the supplying of their legitimate wants, their comfort, care, and education, in all stages of life, as well in infancy, sickness, infirmity, and old age; and to be used also to carry out the principles, business, and various objects of the community, in accordance with the purport of an instrument styled, "*Act of Donation to the Icarian Community*" dated April 22d, A. D., 1879, and recorded in Book II., miscellaneous, at page 378, in the office of Recorder of Deeds, Adams County, State of Iowa.

### Section III.—*Duration and Dissolution.*

Art. 4.—The duration of the Icaria-Esperanza commune shall be ninety-nine years, counting from the date of the adoption of this contract, and its organization shall be renewed whenever it becomes necessary.

Art. 5.—If for any reason whatever this contract should become annulled, or if for any cause whatever the Icaria-Speranza commune should be dissolved, its entire property shall be disposed of in the following manner.

*A.* First, all outside creditors shall be paid up and settled with.

*B.* Next, all credits to which the members of the commune shall be individually entitled to, and which sums shall have been entered on the books of the commune, below their individual name, as their exclusive property, shall be paid to them.

*C.* The remainder shall be accounted for, paid over, assigned or transferred in accordance with the several donations that shall have been made to the Icarian Community, a true copy of which donations is hereto attached.

## SECTION IV.—*Capital Stock.*

ART. 6.—The capital stock of the Icaria-Speranza commune comprises all kinds of property, and constitutes a common fund owned by the commune and applicable to all its wants through its proper agents.

But said common fund shall not be mortgaged, alienated or indebted to a greater extent than is hereinafter prescribed, unless nine tenths of the members having voting privilege agree, in general assembly, to such greater alienation.

ART. 7.—The common fund of the Icaria-Speranza commune is composed of all sums of money or property of any description that shall have been either donated, transferred, assigned, or set over in any lawful manner to the commune, by friends, well-wishers, charter-members or later admitted members, by societies or any other communes ; and such money or property, as well as all accumulations thereof, shall be held in trust and used only in accordance with the purport of said donations, transfers, assignments, and the stipulation of this contract.

ART. 8.—The common fund of the Icaria-Speranza commune is further composed of all sums of money or property whatever, owned or possessed by its individual members before entering this association.

But such money or property as shall have been conditionally contributed to the common fund by individual members, is to be refunded to them, in case of their withdrawal from the commune, under such conditions as are hereinafter agreed to.

ART. 9.—However, each and every individual member has the exclusive use and ownership of the following property :

*A.* Each and every article of his wardrobe.

*B.* Each and every article of his furniture, bedding, and household implements.

*C.* Each and every article that shall have been given him as a present by persons who are not members of the commune, and who shall be still living at the time when the individual member takes possession of such present ; provided, however, that, in the aggregate, the fair value of the present, or presents, so received in the course of any one year, shall not exceed fifty dollars, and that all surplus shall be remitted to the common fund, and entered on the member's credit.

*D.* Each and every article which shall have been given him as a present by any one member or members of the commune, who shall still be living at the time when the donee-member takes possession of such present ; provided, however, that, in the aggregate, the fair value of the present or presents so received by him in the course of any one year shall not exceed twenty-five dollars, and that all surplus shall be remitted to the fund.

### SECTION V.—*Production and Business.*

ART. 10.—The general nature of production and business of the Icaria-Speranza commune is as follows, to wit : agriculture, horticulture, viticulture, mechanical arts, milling, manufacturing, and commerce in all various branches ; also the building and establishing of schools, colleges, villages, colonies, and the developing of sciences and fine arts.

### SECTION VI.—*Administration.*

ART. 11.—The business affairs and common interests generally shall be conducted by a Board of Administration, composed of five committees, denominated as follows :

*A.* Committee on Works.

*B.* Committee on Home-Consumption.

*C.* Committee on Education.

*D.* Committee on Commerce.

*E.* Committee on Accounts.

ART. 12.—Each one of these five committees shall be composed of at least two members having voting privilege ; and when acting separately, shall transact only such business as comes within the limits of their conferred powers.

ART. 13.—The duties, power, and scope of action of each committee shall be defined in special by-laws to be adopted in general assembly.

ART. 14.—When any unusual or contingent matter shall come before any one committee, the latter shall convene the board of administration and lay such matter before them, either for final decision, or for reference to a special or to an ordinary meeting of the general assembly.

ART. 15.—The board of administration may convene the general assembly in extraordinary session, whenever they deem it necessary ; and said board shall convene said assembly when any five members having voting privilege shall have made a written application for that purpose.

ART. 16.—No decision or vote, taken either by a committee or by the board of administration, shall be valid unless it obtains the unanimous assent of its members.

ART. 17.—The title to all common property, either real, personal, or mixed, is vested in the persons composing the board of administration, and in their successors in office, who shall, in this relation, be considered as trustees of the Icaria-Speranza commune.

ART. 18.—Each and every member of the board of administration shall be elected by the general assembly in the month of January, for one year, and shall be, at any time, accountable to, and removable by, said assembly.

ART. 19.—The names of the persons composing the board of administration until next January are as follows, to wit :

### Section VII.—*Liabilities.*

ART. 20.—The highest amount of debts for which the property of the Icaria-Speranza commune shall become liable is thirty-three per cent. of the whole assets, as shall be yearly shown by a correct inventory. For exceptions, see Art. 6.

ART. 21.—The aggregate of debts, or the liabilities of any kind, shall include all credits which may, at any time, become due to the members, as shall appear from the books of the commune.

### Section VIII.—*General Assembly.*

ART. 22.—The general assembly is composed of all members, of both sexes, who are at least twenty-one years old, and who shall have been admitted to sign this contract.

ART. 23.—Minor members above fourteen years of age, and provisional members may be admitted to its sessions, but with consultative voice only.

ART. 24.—Its regular sessions are held semi-annually, but special sessions may be convoked according to the foregoing provisions.

ART. 25.—The general assembly may adopt, at any time, such by-laws and regulations as shall be deemed necessary to the proper fulfilment of this agreement.

ART. 26.—No decision or vote taken in general assembly shall be valid unless carried by fully three fourths of the voting members who shall be present at the session when such vote is taken.

ART. 27.—A majority of fully three fourths of the members having voting privilege constitutes a " quorum," without which " quorum " the general assembly shall not open its sessions, except to adjourn twice, if necessary ; and, after such adjournments, a majority of half plus one of the members having voting privilege shall be deemed a " quorum " to transact any business.

ART. 28.—All admissions of new members, all expulsions of members, and all elections to any office shall be by ballot upon unsigned tickets.

ART. 29. Elections to any office shall not be valid, unless carried as follows, to wit :—

*A.* Candidates must obtain a majority of fully three fourths of the members having voting privilege, to be elected on first ballot.

*B.* Elections on second ballot shall be determined by a majority of half-plus-one of the members having voting privilege.

*C.* A relative majority, viz. : the highest number of votes cast, shall carry an election on third ballot.

SECTION IX.— *Withdrawal Fund.*

ART. 30.—In the month of January of every year, the board of administration, through the committee on accounts, shall make a correct inventory in which every article of common property of the Icaria-Speranza commune shall be listed and appraised at its fair cash value.

ART. 31.—In appraising some classes of property, especially real estate, the possible fluctuation of the market shall be taken into consideration, and the average fair cash value, of such property, in two or more past years, shall be deemed the correct value.

Art. 32.—One of the objects of the taking of said inventory is to fairly ascertain the surplus or net profit earned, year after year, by the Icaria-Speranza commune, said profit to be expressed in dollars.

Art. 33.—When the amount of said surplus shall have been ascertained, and approved by the general assembly, said amount shall be divided into two halves ; one half shall belong to the commune and accumulate to the common fund ; and the other half shall be divided by the number of members having the voting privilege for the purpose of ascertaining each member's equal share.

Art. 34.—The amount thus yearly found due to each member shall be entered on the books of the commune, below his individual name, together with any other credits that he may have ; but shall only become his exclusive property, and be paid him, in case of his withdrawal from the commune.

### Section X.—*Consideration.*

Art. 35.—Besides all other benefits that each member may derive from this contract, the Icaria-Speranza commune, as a further consideration, shall enter on its books, and pass to the credit side of each individual member having voting privilege, the sum of two hundred dollars, to come out of its property, and to be paid to said member in case of his withdrawal ; provided, however, that each such member shall have made a donation, transfer, or assignment forever of his property to the Icaria-Speranza commune, located at near Cloverdale, Sonoma County, State of California, within one year from the date of the recording of this contract, or, previously to such recording, to the Icarian Community situated near Corning, Adams County, State of Iowa.

### Section XI.—*Labor Premiums.*

Art. 36.—Monthly labor premiums shall be given to each member, being above sixteen years of age, provided said member partakes in the common work of the commune ; said premium shall be paid in money, and shall not be less than fifty cents, nor more than one dollar and a half per month.

Art. 37.—The member of the board of administration, acting as treasurer, shall not pay any money as labor premiums, unless in accordance with the following conditions :

*A.* Every month he shall pay a premium of fifty cents to each member who shall not have lost more than one working-day during said month.

*B.* Every month he shall pay a premium of one dollar to each member who shall not have lost more than half a working-day during said month.

*C.* No excuse whatever shall be admitted as a substitute for working-time lost by a member, in relation to the payment of premiums.

Art. 38.—The general assembly shall adopt a special by-law in which all labor of any kind that is to be considered common work, shall be defined.

### Section XII.—*Inheritance.*

Art. 39.—Each and every signer of this contract formally agrees and stipulates that if he deceases while being a member, each and every article of his individual property, as well as all credits entered on the books of the commune, shall return forthwith to the common fund ; with such minimum exception, however, as the law may require.

### Section. XIII.—*Clothing.*

Art. 40.—The board of administration, through the committee on home consumption, shall make a semi-annual budget of expenses necessary to properly clothe each and every member of the Icaria-Speranza commune, and to that effect they shall carry out the following rule :

*A.* They shall ascertain and express in dollars what sum is necessary to purchase the clothing, in the six ensuing months, of each full-grown female member.

*B.* They shall find what sum is necessary for each full-grown male member.

*C.* They shall classify all the children in as many series as shall be found necessary, and ascertain what sum is wanted to clothe each member of each series.

*D.* When the aggregate of all such sums shall be found, they shall submit the " Semi-Annual Budget of Expenses for Clothing " to the general assembly for correction or approval.

*E.* After such proceedings, the member of the board of administration, acting as delegate to commercial business, shall open, in one or more stores of the nearest town to be designated by said delegate, a credit to each individual member, said credit not to exceed the sum found as his individual budget ; and the said delegate shall see, when necessary, that no credits opened in any store are diverted from their legitimate destination.

*F.* All credits so opened shall be equal for each member of each series of persons ; but in cases of special wants of clothing for special common works, or common purposes, the committee on home consumption may cause such articles to be bought and delivered whenever deemed necessary, and every such article shall be common property to be used temporarily.

ART. 41.—Within the limits of his individual budget, each member shall be at liberty to select whatever object of clothing that suits him.

SECTION XIV.—*Rights and Duties.*

ART. 42.—All who shall be admitted to sign this contract, together with their children, shall be members of the Icaria-Speranza commune, and shall have equally all the same rights and privileges, either express or implied, pertaining to such membership ; provided, however, that no privilege, so exercised by any one member, shall conflict with the expressed or implied provisions of this contract.

ART. 43.—The committee on home consumption shall see that all food prepared and cooked in the common kitchen be wholesome, and that the menu, or bill of fare, be so varied and so complete as is reasonably compatible with the means of the commune.

ART. 44.—As far as practicable and not objectionable, all meals shall be taken in common, in the common dining-room of the commune ; but each member shall have the privilege to obtain, from the menu prepared in the common kitchen, his reasonable proportion of food, and to take his meals wherever he pleases.

ART. 45.—In cases of sickness each member shall be entitled to a private bill of fare, privately prepared, provided said bill shall not exceed the ordinary and reasonable staples of food, and call only for such articles of food as shall be within the easy purchasing powers of the commune.

Art. 46.—Except in special cases designated by the general assembly, each member shall reside on the place where the commune is located, in houses furnished for that purpose ; and said residences shall only be used for their legitimate destination, viz.: exclusively as dwellings for said members.

Art. 47.—Each and every signer hereof formally agrees and stipulates that he shall never claim, nor attempt to recover, either directly or indirectly, at law or in equity, any other sums of money, or property whatever, than is herein specified and provided for as part of the compensation given by the commune for his time, services and labor.

Art. 48.—He further agrees and stipulates that he relinquishes all rights of recovery from work, time, or services whatever given to the commune, by any one member of his family ; relinquishing also all rights of recovery either for services, damages, expectancy of life or estate, in cases of death or of any accident whatever that may have happened, by any reason or cause, to any one or every member of his family ; agreeing hereby that the benefits that he, and each member of his family, derived daily from the operations of this contract, are ample and sufficient compensation for the relinquishment of all such rights.

Art. 49.—Each and every member of this association shall give his entire working time and abilities to the common use and works of the commune, as shall be amicably distributed among them by the committee on works, after a workers' consultation.

Art. 50.—The Icaria-Speranza commune shall give to each minor member, at least until he shall have attained the age of sixteen years, as thorough and as complete an education, in both English and French languages, as shall be found reasonably compatible, at any time, with the various works, the financial means, and the professorial opportunities of the association.

Section XV.—*Admission.*

Art. 51.—New members may be admitted in the Icaria-Speranza

commune, and allowed to sign this contract, under the following conditions :

*A.* Each and every applicant for admission should sufficiently know the French language to speak it and read it fluently.

*B.* All admissions shall be, at first, provisional, and shall not be valid, unless fully nine tenths of the members having voting privilege, assent, by a vote in general assembly, to such provisional admission.

*C.* After such provisional admission, each applicant shall stay in novitiate for a term of strictly twelve consecutive months, after which term he may be absolutely admitted in general assembly, by a vote of fully nine tenths of the members having voting privilege.

ART. 52.—Upon the written request of five voting members, the board of administration may cause any provisional member, as well as any other person having sojourned for more than three consecutive days, to withdraw from the commune at any time within forty-eight hours from such request.

SECTION XVI.— *Withdrawals.*

ART. 53.—After having given ten days' notice of his intention to the committee on accounts, each member may, at any time, resign his membership and withdraw from the commune, but such formal resignation shall be made on a written and signed instrument stating that the resigning member relinquishes all his membership rights for the purpose of obtaining a settlement of his accounts with the commune.

ART. 54.—After such proceedings, the committee on accounts shall convene the board of administration, and lay before them such letter of resignation for final acceptation and mode of settlement of the resigner's account, or for reference to the general assembly.

ART. 55.—Within sixty days after he shall have tendered his resignation, each member shall receive, and be paid, all his credits that shall have been entered on the books of the commune ; provided, however, that within the twelve months preceding such resignation, the Icaria-Speranza commune shall not have paid out, as fund for withdrawing members, more than fifteen hundred dollars in the aggregate.

ART. 56.—When within any one year the Icaria-Speranza commune shall have paid to withdrawing members a sum of money exceeding fifteen hundred dollars, the board of administration, when requested to settle with any other resigning member, shall strike a balance of the account of said member, deliver him a due-bill or note for such balance, and shall be allowed one year's time to pay said bill.

Art. 57.—In cases of married members, the resignation of the husband shall imply the resignation of his wife, and *vice versâ ;* as well as of all their children under sixteen years of age.

## Section XVII.—*Expulsions.*

Art. 58.—When the conduct, or general behavior, of any member above sixteen years of age shall be so obnoxious as to seriously endanger either the material, financial, or moral interests of the Icaria-Speranza commune, he may be ousted from his membership and expelled from the commune.

Art. 59.—Each accused member shall have ten days' notice of the charges preferred against him, and shall have fair opportunities to defend himself in general assembly ; but no expulsion shall be valid unless carried by a vote of fully nine tenths of the members having voting privilege, the vote to be expressed in two different sessions, to be held at least thirty days from the first.

Art. 60.—No member, or his wife, and *vice versâ*, shall vote upon his own expulsion ballot, and in case he does vote, his ticket shall be refused.

Art. 61.—The expulsion of a member husband shall imply the resignation of his wife, and *vice versâ ;* as well as the resignation of all their children under sixteen years of age.

## Section XVIII.—*Revisions.*

Art. 62.—Each and every article of this contract may be revised in General Assembly ; but the revision of any article shall not be valid unless the following rules shall have been strictly adhered to :

*A.* The unanimous consent by vote is requisite to revise the following enumerated Articles : 1, 2, 3, 4, 5, 6, 7,—30, 31, 32, 33, 34, 35,—42, 43, 44, 45, 46, 47, 48, 49, and 50.

*B.* The consent by vote of fully nine tenths of the members having voting privilege is requisite to revise the following enumerated Articles : 8, 9,—20, 21, 22, 23,—39,—53, 54, 55, 56, 57, 58, 59, 60, 61, 62.

*C.* The consent by vote of three fourths of the members having voting privilege is requisite to revise the following enumerated Articles : 10, 11, 12, 13, 14, 15, 16, 17, 18, 19,—24, 25, 26, 27, 28, 29,—36, 37, 38,—40, 41.

*D.* The consent by vote of nine tenths of the members is requisite to revise Articles 51 and 52 ; but after a period of three years, from the day of recording of this contract, Articles 51 and 52 shall be revisable by a majority of three fourths of the members having voting privilege.

# INDEX.

217

# THE AMERICAN UTOPIAN ADVENTURE

sources for the study of communitarian socialism in the
United States 1680–1880

## Series One